P9-DFP-490

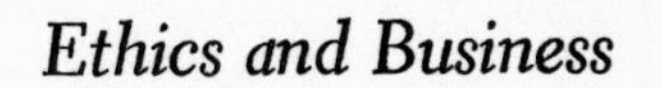
Ethics and Business

ETHICS and BUSINESS

William A. Spurrier

CHARLES SCRIBNER'S SONS
New York

A-9.62[V]

PRINTED IN THE UNITED STATES OF AMERICA

Library of Congress Catalog Card Number 62-16656

TO DAVID M. HUNT

Who is first among businessmen I know to practice his business with moral integrity, and who would be the last to make such a claim.

ACKNOWLEDGMENTS

I am indebted to my several friends in the business world who have freely and frankly educated me as to the nature of the problems they face. Among them are: Frank R. Wallace, Jr., Oliver Martin, A. Mason Harlow, Jr., and Manton Copeland, Jr. To my colleague, Professor Kenneth Underwood, I owe much for his stimulating criticisms and insights over the past few years. Special appreciation is due to my secretary Mrs. Patsy Sutherland who deciphered my hieroglyphics and translated them into type. Finally, to my wife I owe more than I can say, especially for putting up with the pre-occupied mind and stare which seem to appear when a manuscript is in process!

William A. Spurrier

Contents

Ethics and Business

Introduction

This little book, written in the form of a series of letters, is addressed to sensitive businessmen who are concerned about Christianity and business. This volume is particularly and especially written for those people who have tried sincerely to be something more than "Sunday Christians" but who, nevertheless, really wonder whether one *can* be a Christian *and* a businessman at the same time. Faced with a competitive situation, can one give in and "go the second mile"? Is forgiveness possible to one's competitor? How can one love and still make a profit? These and many other questions arise in the sensitive conscience. And many men have gone to church hoping to find some help in relating their Christian Faith to their everyday business decisions. But they come away each Sunday with a sigh for they do not receive much help. Part of this is due to clergy who do not know much about economics and business. And part of it is due to laymen who ask the wrong questions, or who think there is a simple sentence somewhere in the Bible which will provide an absolutely right answer for any specific business decision.

This book is also partly directed to those businessmen who feel that it is a relatively easy thing to be a good Christian and a good businessman at the same time. It is the conviction of this author that such is not the case, that both Christianity and business are much more complicated and profound, and that one cannot make such an easy identification of faith and virtue.

On the whole, however, the deeper issue is not the particular inadequacies of clergy and businessmen, but rather the failure to understand the nature of our Christian Faith and the failure of serious communication between clergy and businessmen. These letters, addressed to imaginary people, try to deal with real issues. As with all letters, there are limitations. For instance, it is difficult to include any two-way conversation; this is true of most regular books also. But this form of letter writing has been chosen to emphasize the need for further communication and conversation between concerned Christians, and also because it is to be hoped that these letters might even be used as a basis for discussion among various groups of people.

It is obvious that each letter deals with only a sample problem and offers only some sample answers. No one letter, nor all taken together, should even be considered the whole story about Christianity and its application to business problems. This volume, then, is an attempt to begin an explanation of Christianity's relation to business and to start the communication so needed from the clergy side of the fence (pew?).

— 1 —

Mr. John Richards
Main Street
Middle City, U.S.A.

Dear Mr. Richards:

Thank you for your most interesting and discerning letter. I think you are right when you say that today the American businessman's image or picture in the eyes of the public is blurred or painted by contradictory brushes. Happily, the old picture of the businessman as the fat cat from Wall Street, or the silk-hatted money bag with his foot on the back of the poor is now passé or left to the marxists. There is no doubt, I think, that most businessmen are as moral and immoral as the rest of us. And over-all, there has developed a sense of public responsibility among many executives. Further, many sincere Christians and others are constantly struggling to relate their religious faith to their everyday business life. I agree with you when you say we have come a long way from the days of the Robber Barons. It is just not true to kick the businessman around as if he were some kind of special moral leper, worse than the rest of society.

On the other hand, I think you might agree with me that there are some dangers on the other side of the coin. I get a little annoyed when someone says that he runs his business according to the Golden Rule, or that the Sermon on the Mount really works. Aren't you a little suspicious when a company says that their only concern is public service? Nobody is *that* good! And of course, there are all kinds of other reminders of our moral feet of clay: conflict of interests examples, bribes, favors, etc.

What I am trying to say is that the contemporary cultural view of the businessman is an ambiguous one, partly caused by businessmen themselves and partly by others. Conscious of the early obvious immorality of big business, the contemporary businessman has tried to become more moral, more socially responsible. Compared to the early 1900's he has succeeded. On the other hand, he is now in danger of appearing to be more righteous than he really is. The problem of self-deception is very difficult and very subtle. Because I do not commit an obvious wrong, I am tempted to believe that therefore I am obviously good. And if you think I think that this problem is limited to businessmen, let me add what you know but have been too polite to say, namely, that this is *the* problem of the parson. This is, of course, Pharisaism. And we clergy are susceptible to this especially, precisely because it seems that we are doing such obvious good works. Therefore, we are so likely to imagine that we are obviously good. Anyway, Pharisaism is our common problem. We are not as good as we think we are.

From the public's side, you businessmen face another difficult problem. Some people think that you are the Saviours of America not because you are Saints, but because you are practical, tough activists. What we need, they say, is less talk and more action. And it's the businessman who can act efficiently and quickly and not get bogged down in theory and complexity. Well, of course, we all want efficiency and practical action. But action for what? More goods, more profit? Yes—but then what? No matter where you drop in on the "what," you raise theoretical and practical questions of value. So this racing around doing things efficiently and tough-mindedly can be quite useless unless we know what ends and values we are trying to achieve.

Of course, the opposite is equally true and I believe you pointed it out in one of your previous letters, namely, there is a limit to theory too. Clergy and professors spend a lot of time analyzing and theorizing, introducing one complexity after another, and then often end up with a noble resolution! But who *does* anything about it? So businessmen and many laymen listen to us, and then how you yearn for a man of action! "Never mind the yak-yak, let's *do* something" is the understandable reaction.

Well, you can see what I'm driving at. It's really a question of balance, of both/and, or better, a marriage of theory and action. Any organization needs brain men and action men, and it's great when you can find that combination in one man, but it's fairly rare. I've always liked the reply of Harold Ickes back in the New Deal days. Never mind the political arguments pro and con now. But do you remember when he was hauled before a Congressional Committee investigating something or other? Ickes was attacked pretty strongly because he was a "Brain Truster," a "big think man" and so on. To which Ickes replied, "Gentlemen, is there some other part of the anatomy which you think is better qualified to deal with problems?"

So there is this image of the hard-headed practical businessman who will solve all problems without too much trouble, talk and theory. But I have the feeling that not many of you really believe this. Some do, of course, but I suspect it is the non-business person, or the little man on the way up who believes this image. I trust you will edify them as to the facts of the problem.

There is another image of the businessman which, I believe, is more widespread and pervasive. This is the public view that most of you are materialists, not predatory or crass ones, but nevertheless, concerned only with profits and things. Your life is consumed by the desire to make a profit and have a lot of comforts in life and all else is secondary. To be sure, you are fairly enlightened: you make overtures to keeping the employees happy, in keeping America strong (on a cost plus basis), and hollering about freedom and democracy (meaning: leave me alone to make a profit, but bail me out when I don't). Some image that! What do you think of the picture? As for me, I think it is fairly but not wholly true. But I would add that I think this is a picture of *all* of us, not just businessmen. What is the basic difference between a man whose installment debt per annum is $3,000 and the corporation executive who drives himself and his staff to increase their profit from 6¼ to 6½ percent? I say there is no difference. Both men are after something they don't really need, their primary target is either status, or status by having things, or power, or power over things. But don't get me started on this "materialism." I could write a long, long chapter on it. Suffice it to say now that I do believe we are all over-attached to action and accumulation of goods and things. On the other hand, I do not believe that material things are evil in themselves. I find nothing in the Biblical faith which says that the spirit is good and matter evil. Things are basically good, but like all things, they can be used or misused. All I'm saying is that I do think we Americans are partly misusing our things by being too attached to them, too dependent upon them, and too worshipful about them. Most young people that I know, for instance, really believe that if and when they get the right job with the adequate salary, a good house and a good wife, then they will be completely happy. To which I always reply, "Are the people on Park Avenue more happy than those in Levittown? Ask the psychoanalysts." I am not saying that poverty is the road to happiness. But it is a question not only of balance but of primary loyalty to what values. And these we will deal with later. But for now, I am merely calling to your attention some of the images of the businessmen that are prevalent in the U.S. today.

In closing, then, what I would like to do is to try to give a summary of what seems to me to be a basic cultural problem for all of us. The image businessmen have of themselves alternates between too good a picture and a too narrow view. Most Chamber of Commerce portrayals, for instance, disclose both at the same time. You are painted as giants of the earth endowed with practical, active wisdom, who are the only true patriots, and who at the same time are the only ones who can operate the economy of business successfully—that is, as business goes so goes the country. This is an extreme picture, of course, but I believe it is mostly true in varying degrees in the business community. There are many exceptions, naturally. Indeed, privately, many like you would say that your problem is the opposite. You are not giants of the earth. Quite the contrary, you are very average men struggling with very tough problems, haunted by complexities, moral ambiguities, and a hunger for finding some meaning in it all. This I believe is also true, but it is not the published image. And this is the point: you have to live with both the public and private image of yourself and you wonder whether it is possible.

Then to make things more difficult there is the popular image of the businessman. This portrayal also fluctuates in opposite directions. One view sees you, admiringly, as the backbone of America; the other picture paints you as a tough, smart, fairly enlightened entrepreneur out to make a pile of money and let everyone else look out. A minority view has a much more dismal portrait, namely that you are hypocrites, not always consciously. But you are basically grubbing materialists while pretending to be stalwart pillars of the moral community. You know the old joke: you go to church on Sunday and fleece the consumer or competitor on Monday (legally, of course). So there is the popular image a bit overstated. And how do you live with or combat these pictures?

My thoughts for this letter are something like this: First, all the images are partly right. Therefore we will get nowhere by denying them. Second, it is useless to counter one image with the opposite image. This only results in a battle of stereotypes with each side making more ridiculous claims for itself, thereby making the image more fatuous. Third, it is also useless to say, "I will be myself and do what I have to do and ignore public opinion." This doesn't work because what is myself? What kind of a person am I? I may be a hypocrite. I may be too materialistic. Or I may be a man of integrity and public responsibility. Or, more likely, I probably am a fabulous mixture of egoism, morality, immorality, sensitivity, anxiety and what not. The problem is: how do I know what I am, honestly, and where do I stand and what ought I to do? Fourth, in order to judge myself and these cultural images, I need a perspective which is greater than and truer than me and the culture. This is where Christianity comes in. One central message of the Law and the prophets, one basic message of Christ and the New Testament was judgment, not condemnation, but judgment. Judgment means criticism—good and bad—from a yardstick, a standard. The standard is not my neighbor, not social custom, not what is legal, not even noble ideals; the standard is God. All else is relative to Him.

Well, I must not go on now. But this is what I hope to spell out in our future letters. Of course it is too easy just to say, "God is our first loyalty, our ultimate standard and Reality." The real issue is to show how God is relevant to our daily living and business decisions and policies. Naturally, I do not know all the answers either. But with your patience and understanding, I hope I can offer some guides and some partial answers at least. So bear with me in my future letters as I try to explain how I think the Christian faith *is* relevant to your daily life and mine. And, of course, I will need your views on these problems too.

Relevantly (I hope) yours, etc.

— 2 —

Mr. Edwin Johnson
Hardy's Department Store
Evansville, Indiana

Dear Mr. Johnson:

You ask my response to several basic questions. Your first one is, I think, the most commonly asked. You say, "Why aren't the Ten Commandments, the Golden Rule and the Sermon on the Mount good enough? They are clear, concise and practical. Why do you ministers complicate religion by talking about revelation, resurrection, miracles, justification by faith—whatever that is—sacraments and all that? Why not give us the straight and simple Gospel the way Jesus did?"

Let me first say that I think I can understand your basic feeling that a man's religion ought to be clear, concise and have practical application. And as a clergyman, I must confess to you that we have not always clarified the Christian faith, but have often obscured it. If you are protesting against irrelevant and boring sermons, complicated and abstract theology, I will join you up to a point. I will go whole hog with you against the sermons but only part way on the theology. Somebody has to wrestle with the tough and complicated theoretical problems. Where would atomic physics be today without the abstract seemingly impractical theoreticians like Einstein or Bohr? But if you are saying that such abstruse theory does not belong in the pulpit, I'm with you. So, at the start, I'm agreeing that too many of us parsons have offered you too many dull, or irrelevant, or too theological sermons.

But now let's see what you have really said by taking your suggestions one at a time. Let's take the Ten Commandments. Numbers one and two: "I am the Lord thy God; thou shalt have none other gods but me," and "Thou shalt not make any graven image —nor bow down, nor worship other gods." What do these mean? It is easy to *say* I believe in God. But what do we mean by the word God? For most of us we mean that there is some kind of vague power that makes the world go around, makes life possible and sort of keeps it going. This is a safe belief—nice and general and unspecific and impersonal. It's like saying I believe in natural process, in life itself. Who would disagree? And have we said anything important anyway? Well, it's okay to believe in nature, life and its general processes—we more or less have to or else. But this is obvious and why call it God anyway. Why not just nature and its powers?

More important, what about the worship of false gods? And here we are not talking about golden calves, or totem poles, but about the gods of success, status, money, America, my ego. The Law says thou shalt not worship these gods. But in our more honest moments, I think you will agree with me that we do. Not all of the time—we're not that bad, but a lot of the time—we're not that good. So here is a law and we break it. Proof? What of the businessman who spends most of his energies concentrating on his business and neglects his family, especially his children? What of the minister who does the same thing—worships the job of being a minister and neglects his family and "the weightier matters of the Law"? You are not specially guilty; this is our human condition, the way we are.

Or take another commandment: "Thou shalt not covet." What does this mean? Does it mean you should not want to win that competitive bid? Is it wrong to want to get promoted, wrong to want a new car, a better house? The Ten Commandments do not easily explain themselves. If you or I say it is not wrong to want nice things, by what authority do we say that this is *not* coveting, or that it is? You see the point. The Commandments are apparently simple statements, but how shall we interpret and apply them? This is where complexity and difficulty come in. Incidentally, this is where theology comes in. Part of theology *is* interpretation and application. So here we are amateur theologians right on the practical issue. Is it coveting to want the good things in life? The Commandments do not tell us.

So let's turn to the Golden Rule: "Do unto others as you would have them do unto you." Well again, what does this mean and how shall we apply it? For example, I want to sell more goods than my competitor; I want to win. Does the Rule then mean that I should let the competitor win so that he, in turn, would let me win? Or does it mean that we both should struggle fairly and efficiently and then hope I win? Or what if he cuts corners legally or otherwise and thereby wins? Shall I retaliate in kind? or shall I remain a nice guy. But what if "nice guys finish last?" And the problem gets even more complicated when we realize that what I want done to me may *not* be the same as I want to do for others. I want to get ahead, I don't want to lose. Everybody can't be a leader or an executive or a vice president. True, but let's make sure that I do. Now what happens to the Golden Rule here? Like so many little maxims and ethical ditties, this Rule has a partial use. It is a simple guidepost that is practical in some simple situations. Don't hit a fellow on the jaw over an argument about a bridge hand or golf shot. You wouldn't want him to hit you, so don't hit him. In short, the Golden Rule is a common sense maxim for simple situations. But it is quite irrelevant and inadequate for difficult situations in everyday life.

And thirdly, let's look at the Sermon on the Mount. But before we get involved in this, here's a little test you might try on your friends sometime. The next time someone says to you, "I believe in the Sermon on the Mount," ask him what the Sermon says, *what* is contained in it. I think you will be surprised how few people really know what it does say. So let's look at it.

In the first place, the Sermon on the Mount was not a Sermon and was not given on a mountain. The "Sermon" is a collection of some of the sayings of Jesus. This collection made it easier for people to hear or read and then pass the sayings on to someone else. Similarly today, we have short collections of some of the speeches of Abraham Lincoln, F.D.R. and Eisenhower. But more important, what did Jesus say?

The first part of the collection is the Beatitudes. "Blessed are the peace makers, the poor in spirit, those who hunger and thirst after righteousness, the merciful," etc. Here Jesus is describing blessed attitudes. And I think you will agree with me that such attitudes are indeed saintly, almost holy. In fact, so high and pure that none of us can say we really achieve them. They may be something to shoot for as an ideal and thereby act as a kind of yardstick or judge on our lesser motives and attitudes. In any case, the Beatitudes deal with our inner motives and it is difficult to see how one relates these to business. I personally believe there *is* a relationship, but it is not an obvious or an easy one. And I shall try to show later what the relationship might be; meanwhile, no one is likely to replace the "Think" signs in his office with one of the Beatitudes.

The rest of the Sermon on the Mount and the chief substance

of it deals primarily with three major points: the necessity and desirability of Love, Faith, and Prayer. The kind of love Jesus describes is precisely the most difficult and seemingly impractical kind of all. "Love your enemies," "go the second mile," "forgive seventy times seven," "pray for those who persecute you." In short, this love is sacrificial, spontaneous, does not seek rewards, it is universal and so applies to all, friend and foe alike, it seeks to reconcile enemies. If we think the Beatitudes are saintly, what about this kind of love? I cannot speak for you, but I know that when somebody irritates (not even persecutes) me, my natural reaction is to be irritable towards him. I do not find myself praying for enemies; I think about how to beat them or get back at them. If someone beats you out on a deal fairly or not, do you really rejoice for him? When you really see what Jesus said, I think we must acknowledge that His Love is well beyond us. It is God's Love and we do not have it naturally. Therefore, it is really pretentious to claim that we do have this kind of love and that we run our business by it. The fact is we don't; we're not that good.

Next, look at faith. Clearly Jesus did not mean that we can trust our own abilities or have faith that everything will work out all right if we just keep trying and are sincere. Valid self-confidence has its place, along with effort and integrity. But these things are not faith. Faith, in the New Testament, is an active commitment to the God that Jesus described and illustrated, indeed, to the God that was disclosed in Christ. What does this mean? It means that one's first and most basic desire and trust is "to seek the kingdom (power) of God first," that is, a man of Christian Faith prays that God's power will come to him and operate through him. He seeks to find the God of Jesus Christ in the market place, at the office, in the home and to relate all things to Him. That is what faith means: committing our whole person to this Reality we call God.

Again, it should be obvious that none of us do commit our whole person to God. Most of the time we commit nothing, and part of the time, we commit part of ourselves—the well-intentioned Sunday part or the fast office prayer before we give the bad news to our assistant. It is no accident, then, that the last part of the "Sermon" deals with prayer. Since we are not good enough and do not have enough faith, we need to seek communion with God and open ourselves up to His power. Prayer is one of the chief avenues to God, and God to us. In the Sermon, Jesus did not explain a great deal about prayer. There he primarily called for integrity and sincerity in prayer, rather than outward group performances just to show off one's religiosity. That is the substance of the Sermon on the Mount.

So I would ask, "Now what has that got to do with running a business?" For me, I can see no simple connection, no easy practical application. When a fellow says he runs his business by the Sermon on the Mount, I just have to conclude that he doesn't know what the Sermon says, or else he is just deceiving himself. Actually, in most cases, I believe men are sincere when they say things like this. But I believe they have used a cliché without really thinking about it. It is time, I think, to stop using the Sermon on the Mount as a slogan. To use the Sermon that way is some new kind of insult to God. To be reduced to a cliché—what a fate for the Almighty and His Son! What an indictment of us!

You'll pardon the strong statements, I hope. It's the only way I can state my convictions and make the point without beating around the bush. And I expect you to reply in kind if you so wish. But the conclusion should be obvious now, namely, that nobody runs his business or the rest of his life by the Ten Commandments, the Golden Rule, and the Sermon on the Mount. We may try but we do not succeed. And it is a matter of basic honesty and integrity to admit that we do not succeed. If we then go on to say that trying is good enough, then we will run into the fact that trying to apply the Commandments and the Sermon is extremely difficult, complex and possibly impractical. So much so, that we shall be always tempted to say that, alas the ideals are too high, too impractical and the world is too tough for them.

I conclude by quoting from a friend of mine who said, "The simple Gospel is not as simple as some simple people simply think."

Unsimply yours, etc.

— 3 —

MR. GEORGE VINSON
AMERICAN ASSOCIATION OF MANUFACTURERS
NEW YORK CITY

Dear Mr. Vinson:

Your frank and blunt letter arrived yesterday. After spending the night recovering from your bombs and direct hits, I shall try to respond! Let me say that I appreciate your blunt approach: it makes the issues clear. And I, for one, do not equate frankness with discourtesy or hostility. So on with our correspondence.

You say, "What's wrong with ideals? How can we live without the ideals of freedom, democracy and honesty? And religiously speaking, how can we live without the ideals of the Ten Commandments, love and justice? Of course, we do not achieve them perfectly or realize them in toto. But is that any reason for abandoning them, or making them irrelevant? I say we need them, they are true, our country was made great by them, and we shall only survive if we keep them before us as our guides. Now what's wrong with that?"

My reply, Mr. Vinson, might be entitled "The Peril of Idealism." I concur that ideals, secular and religious, are necessary. I believe in all the ones you list and many more. I most certainly agree also that we never achieve our ideals and that this is no excuse for discarding them or regarding them as irrelevant. So let's hold on to them and keep trying to approximate them. But now I invite you to consider what happens when we adopt this approach.

I say two chief reactions occur. One, in the struggle to achieve and maintain ideals many people end up believing that they have achieved their ideals, not absolutely perfectly perhaps, but near enough. They tend to equate the achievement of ideals with some obvious example. For instance, if I don't tell any bald-faced lies all day, I can quite easily say I am honest. But what about the shades of gray examples? In my advertising department, do I see that the ads tell the whole truth, or only part of it? How much is slanted, how much plays upon the consumer's fears, or status, or sexuality? Or, do I tell the whole truth to the man I hire or fire, or just the pleasant parts? Or again, what if honesty conflicts with another ideal, say loyalty, or love, or patriotism? Shall I tell the blunt truth to my dying wife, that she is dying of cancer? Shall I be honest and turn in my associate friend who I know is cheating on his income tax? And shall I admit I was spying for my country and tell my captors what I know? In such cases, what shall we do about honesty and our claim to being honest?

I'm arguing that many people unconsciously know that they are not or cannot be always honest. But to admit this is to acknowledge both the limit of ideals and the guiltiness of ourselves. To avoid this failure and guilt, we then proceed to parade our clear-cut achievements of simple honesty. And at the same time we can fortify our virtues by pointing out that we do not do a lot of obviously evil things. We do not commit murder, theft, extortion, bribery, therefore we are obviously good, moral people. But are we so good in the tough complex and ambiguous situations?

I would also call to your attention other examples. How many of us equate freedom with free enterprise, individual independence with rugged go-gettingness? How free is oleomargerine to compete with butter? How much do we really believe in free competition from foreign competitors? How much do we rail against government interference or spending, but welcome the disguised subsidy either in tax write-offs, or outright gifts? And are all critics of some of our short-comings necessarily socialists, leftists or Commies? If you take my loaded questions in this paragraph, I bet your first reaction was: "He's a long-haired professor socialist." Well, it happens that I believe in a mixed free enterprise economic system. A mixture of freedom and social responsibility. What the right mixture is, I am convinced, is the legitimate area of debate and criticism. And I am sure that the mixture will always be fluid and dynamic.

I am saying, then, that some businessmen have a fixed and static view of free enterprise, which they equate with freedom, and anything to the contrary is wrong and against freedom. And I would further say that many socialists and all marxists err in the opposite direction. They equate social progress with a closed system and a closed mind. Therefore, anyone who disagrees with them must be a moss-back right winger or a filthy capitalist. I say both are wrong because they believe the ideal is exclusively theirs and only they have or will achieve it.

Because American democracy is obviously more free than Chinese communism or our economic system more productive than India's, does not mean all is well with us. Let us not adopt false modesty or the role of the cynic and say we have nothing worthwhile. But let us not imagine that if only everybody were as good as we the Kingdom would be here.

Is it not true, Mr. Vinson, that a large part of our culture does not really permit us to admit failure? In business, are we not always trying to prove that we are successful, able and competent? Do we not find it very difficult to deal with failure, to tolerate it, let alone to take time to help the man who errs? Granted you can't run a business (or anything else) on incompetent failures, nevertheless, do we not exert enormous pressure for unqualified success and thereby tempt all of us to prove that we do not really fail?

Or take politics, is it not true that neither party can ever afford to say it really made a mistake? Take any administration you want: it is very difficult to find anyone up top who publicly told the nation that this or that policy was wrong. Instead, we go through the most fantastic gyrations to prove that every policy was the right one. I say much of our culture is a success culture which does not really accept imperfection. This makes liars of us all.

One peril of idealism, then, is that it leads many people to a fatuous self-righteousness. I speak with feeling on this because this is the greatest danger in religion as well. Because we are religious, we are thereby the more tempted to feel that we are the righteous ones. This is spiritual pride. And according to Jesus, this is the worst pride of all. If I say I believe in love and justice and God as ideals, it is all too easy to think that I am vastly superior to the egotist, the materialist, and the atheist. I am tempted to say that it is *they* who are the enemies of virtue, freedom, love and progress. It is *they* who are holding us back, while I the noble but unappreciated idealist am the righteous remnant, and the real hope of mankind. This is what the Pharisees said about Jesus: He was a *they*. And so the final ironic tragedy was that the Pharisees killed the Good man in the name of the Good believing the Good was thereby preserved. The first peril of idealism is self-righteousness.

The second peril of idealism is the discouraged abandonment of ideals. When one takes ideals seriously, he knows that he always falls short of them. Further, the higher the ideal, the wider our gap of failure. And if we take the ideal really seriously, then we feel guilty. I may try to avoid guilt by declaring that I am only human, everybody makes mistakes and so on. But deep down inside I still feel guilty. And if you take a really high ideal like forgiving and reconciling love such as Jesus called for, then we really do fail and the ideal does seem far removed from the hurly-burly world of Madison Avenue or Main Street. And so it is that many conscientious and sincere people have started out with some set of noble ideals and have soon discovered they cannot achieve them and that they stand judged and guilty. It is then so easy and natural and human to conclude that ideals are true and noble and high, but alas, they are futile. How many people have abandoned Christianity, for instance, because they regarded it as only a high ideal of love? I suspect that most people have given up this ideal of love regretfully, nostalgically, reluctantly. They wish this kind of love were possible. But they know that this is a demanding, egoistic and competitive life, and that one must look out for himself and his own, or lose out in the struggle. And so they tuck away the ideal love, bringing it out occasionally in some obvious charity situation, but believing it is impossible and irrelevant in most daily situations. Thus, people abandon the noble ideal and adopt a lower and more realistic and practical ethic such as "enlightened self-interest" or some other cliché answer.

If you need an illustration of the disillusioned idealist, seek out a cynic. Most cynics I know were once ardent idealists—and some of them, at base, still are. But their response to almost every issue in life is defeatist, sour and often bitter. The chief reason for their response is that from any high ideal standard, any present choice is filled with evil and imperfection, and any proposed solution is obviously only one little step higher or lower. "So," they say, "why get all excited about peace and justice and freedom and equality—we'll never have it. Life is tough, and men deceive themselves with noble and futile illusions." Scratch a cynic and you'll find an ex-idealist. But I must confess that I find most cynics or sceptics quite honest, rigorously so. That is, they really do face up to evil and tragedy in life and to their own imperfections and failures. On this score, they are to be preferred to self-righteous idealists.

I suspect about now, Mr. Vinson, that you are chafing at the bit and ready to argue that you are against both the proud idealist and the cynic, that your position is aware of these two dangers, and that you stand in the middle. Well, if this is true, then let's look at the middle ground which says, "Use the ideals without illusion or despair but keep plugging for them." With this view I would agree. But I would point out that the basic issue now is not whether the ideals are true and relevant, but whether *we* have the power to keep plugging for them. The real place for ideals, as I see it, is this: ideals are necessary. They offer us guidance, judgment and direction. But, by themselves, they do not give us the power to struggle for them. Ideals are static; like yardsticks, they are indispensable for measurement. But there is no power in them.

Thus, I am quite sure you and I could agree on a set of ideals. That is relatively easy. But the problem is one of power. It seems to me that you assume that you have the power inside of you to keep struggling for the ideals. I am saying that I do *not* have such power inside of me. I cannot judge you fairly on this score. I can only speak for myself and from what I have seen in other people. And my conclusion is this: in addition to the pride and abandonment of ideals that I believe is common, I find it is possible to struggle for ideals for awhile. But when any crucial issue arises, the ideals take a beating. For example, in any contest between my ego and my ideals, I'm saying my ego will win out better than ninety percent of the time. And the smarter I am, the more easily I will be able to fool myself into believing that my ideals won out. If I were offered a big job as a big-time professor or minister somewhere, my ego would jump at the chance. Then my intellect would begin thinking up moral reasons why this job would offer "greater opportunities for service" or "a larger chance to witness for Christ." You've seen this happen in your bailiwick, haven't you?

So, if you are wise enough and good enough and loving enough and strong enough to work for your ideals, avoiding pride on the one hand, and cynical futility on the other, then I have no quarrel with you. As for me, I do not believe most of us are this powerful. And this is one reason the Christian faith makes sense to me. It is not a religion of noble ideals. We have libraries full of great plans, noble virtues, and high ideals. If Jesus had only added a couple more, I doubt if we would even know of him today. Instead, the New Testament offers us power—loving, judging, redeeming power. Without this power, it is possible to struggle for ideals so long as we seem to be approaching them. But the nearer we get, the more likely we'll jump to the proud conclusion that we are closer than we really are. Meanwhile, we will probably be pretty rough on those who disagree with us. It is easy to fight for the ideal and be pretty rough on people. Or, if it looks as though we cannot progress towards the ideal, most of us will give up and conclude that the ideal is too high, therefore we better lower our sights and be practical and realistic, or we'll just quit.

So I am as interested in preserving and progressing towards our ideals as you are. But I am saying we can't do it alone. We do not have the power to do it. Therefore we better get the power, and as you can see, this is where, for me, the Christian faith comes in.

Yours for more power, etc.

— 4 —

Mr. Paul Nason
City Club
New City, Colorado

Dear Mr. Nason:

Your kind and thoughtful letter has been received with appreciation and interest. You ask two central questions which seem to me to be very widespread and very important. You inquire about my reactions to "positive thinking" and "enlightened self-interest."

As for "the positive thinking" approach to problems, I regard it as something like an aspirin. It is a sound, practical, effective, and harmless antidote for many minor difficulties. It is a step above the placebos of "Keep Smiling," "Chin Up" and "Be Happy." For the chronic worrier, the mildly self-conscious person, the person feeling slightly inferior, "the power of positive thinking" aspirin is a helpful "guidepost" in dealing with most of the symptoms. But when this "medicine" is regarded as the cure-all for serious and complex problems, it is not good enough.

My chief quarrel with this movement or fad (depending upon one's biases) is not with the aspirin itself, but with the claims made for it. Thus, I get a little irritated if positive thoughts are sold as The Christian faith or *the* answer of both science and religion, or *the* answer in four easy steps to *your* basic needs. Several businessmen I know have told me that they tried this view and tried it sincerely. And they said that they reached bottom very quickly. The positive approach was helpful in terms of a healthy creative attitude about daily routine chores of paper work, personnel work, etc. It was a good antidote to the 11 a.m. let down and the 4 p.m. irritating fatigue trough. But the men were quite strong in pointing out that for the serious, basic policy decisions in their business, for their own deeper anxieties and egoisms, positive thinking is not adequate. Well, I do not think we need to labor the point. I am sure you have discovered the value and limitations of this pill in your own experience and that that is why you asked the question in the first place.

The second question you ask is really much more basic and important: "What's wrong with enlightened self-interest?" By way of response, let me first agree that this view of life, of ethics really, is the most pervasive and widespread in our culture. For all our noble pretensions about the Golden Rule, Ethics, or Judeo-Christian Ethics, I believe that most of us are actually believers and followers of the doctrine of enlightened self-interest. The doctrine runs something like this: The strongest motives in human nature are self-preservation and self-interest. However, civilized rational and educated man knows that one cannot be brutally egoistic. For this would lead to disorder and eventually to a denial of one's own interest. For example, if it is to my self-interest to get some money for my needs, and I then go rob a bank, this is unenlightened. It is stupid because it threatens the order of society and banking, and it will result in my going to jail, and therefore denies my self-interest. The enlightened approach, therefore, is to get a job and make some legitimate money. Thereby, society is enhanced and so is my self-interest.

Now, obviously, such an example is indeed a very simple and a very clean cut one. So the issue is whether most experiences in life are that simple and neat. And you can guess where I stand. Putting it briefly at the start: I would argue that most of life's experiences are quite difficult and complex, and most of our attitudes and motives are very ambiguous and mixed. Thus, the validity of enlightened self-interest depends upon how black and white are our external situations, and how enlightened any of us can really be in fact. Let's analyze first our own possibilities of enlightenment.

I would call to your attention the deep pervasiveness of self-interest. This part of the doctrine I agree with. In Christian theology this inordinate self-interest is part of what we mean by sin. Thus, both the enlightened doctrine and Christian theology agree that self-interest *is* our dominant concern; it is here to stay. But we differ on whether self-interest can be controlled or curbed. Enlightenment assumes that we can edify, educate our self-interest. This is where the doctrine of sin for me enters in to disagree. For, I would have to say that in any real contest between my interests and your interests (or the nation's), I am going to look out for mine first. If I am "enlightened," it only means that I will not wreck you, but I am still going to try to beat you, or ignore you if I can. But now here's the rub, Mr. Nason. I would say that if I am really smart and intelligent, I will be able to dish out a lot of moral talk about kindness to you, service to my society, sacrifice of my own desires for the common good, etc. And I may be so good at this that I will even deceive myself into thinking that what I am doing is really quite unselfish after all. For example, is it not true that most of us say that when we vote in politics we should vote *not* in terms of self-interest, but in terms of what's good for the nation? And is it not true that we think that *we* vote in this enlightened way, but that nobody else does?

Or bring the issue closer to home: as parents, is it not true that we believe we are helping our children in an enlightened way—

only in terms of what is good for them? But how much self-interested pride and ego is mixed in here? We want them to succeed academically and professionally not only for their sake, but for our reputation and status too. As every educator knows, one great problem is to get parents to accept the fact that their children are not as bright as the parents think they are. As parents, do we not vacillate between being over-critical of our children and not critical enough? And can we ever say that our judgment is purely enlightened?

Or, in the field of labor-management conflicts, which side can ever claim it is objective, impartial? Does not each side claim enlightenment for itself and accuse the other of naked self-interest? Does not each side appeal to the enlightened self-interest of the other? "It is to your best interests and the nation's to accept *our* offer." But this does not work. Why? Because both sides know that the other side is not as enlightened as they claim to be, and both sides think that it is the other side which has inordinate, *un*-enlightened self-interest. Both sides accuse the other of self-deception, propaganda, and window dressing. The truth is that both sides are right about the other but not about themselves. And so the conflicts go on with uneasy and temporary truces.

We could go on with countless other examples. But I am sure you see the point. *If* we were sufficiently enlightened, really objective and considerate, enlightened self-interest might work. It is much like saying that if all men were rational we would live rationally. But the fact is that we are not all rational all of the time, and our self-interest is not as enlightened as we think or would like it to be. The doctrine of enlightened self-interest is an idealistic ethic which, as an ideal, isn't too bad, but is incapable of helping us to become enlightened. This, then, is one of the dangers of all idealisms—self-deception. Because I hold high a noble ideal, I am always tempted to believe I come near to achieving it. "Pride goeth before the fall."

But there is another weakness in this doctrine of enlightened self-interest. And here again, it is not so much the doctrine itself, as how it is used. Many of us in our society do not regard enlightenment as an ideal, but as an excuse for predatory self-interest. For example, some of us have become disillusioned with either our own or other people's so-called enlightenment. But we are indeed convinced of everyone's powerful self-interest. So we go on to argue that since everybody is out for what they can get, why shouldn't I get mine? "Self-interest and egoism is the law of life. Let's be realistic and practical. If I don't look out for myself no one else will. God helps those who help themselves." Then we add on to these slogans the following, "Everybody cuts a corner here and there. Nobody is pure. You can't change human nature. If you want to get ahead, you've got to give some favors now and then, pad the expenses a bit; it's expected. You don't get something for nothing." Enlightenment means here the intelligence and cleverness to avoid getting caught, to know when to be scrupulously honest and when to compromise, and to know the difference between what is legally permissible and ethically dubious. And if one is caught with his hand in the till, his defense is usually that "everybody else is doing it, why pick on me?" Or a more subtle defense, an enlightened one, is to claim that one is not responsible for this mistake because, "I didn't know it was the law," or "I was tempted," or was drunk, or it was my Oedipus complex, or the law is an outmoded one. You find "the majority-does-it" argument, for instance, in the Kinsey report. The inference there is that if the majority of people practice certain behavior patterns it is therefore "natural" and good. Any law which is contrary to the majority is therefore obsolete, if not wrong and repressive. The cry then is, "Be modern and enlightened and do away with these silly old conventions and taboos."

Thus, the doctrine of enlightened self-interest can be used cynically to try and justify naked self-interest. So now we are back to the same old problem of the validity and limits of any ideal. Any ideal, be it honesty, service, positive thinking, or enlightened self-interest has a valid place. Ideals define or describe some ideal part of life or some goal or purpose or desirable attitude. And we need such guides. But they are static and have no power. This is why they can be used and misused. This is why, by themselves, they do not meet the basic issue of power. They are aspirins which help, not medicine which cures.

But now it is fair to ask what I do believe about self-interest. For I suspect that most people believe that we parsons are against self-interest and want to replace it by the ideal of love and service. But this is not so for Christians. If we fell for that one, we would simply have offered you another ideal. So let me say again that our doctrine of sin tells us that self-interest is here to stay and we can't get rid of it. Therefore, the basic issue is how to deal with it.

My first suggestion would be to recognize and accept the tremendous power of self-interest in each of us. It is essential that we learn its incredibly deceptive and subtle manifestation, its fabulous mixture of valid self-concern and invalid egoism, and the myriad ways it can disguise itself and make itself morally plausible. There is no one way to learn all this. And this is why introspection, self-criticism, criticism from others, confession, and a standard higher than ourselves, are so essential. And while we are learning, it is safe to assume that we are more egoistic and self-interested than we think we are.

The second suggestion is that we seek a counter power, not an ideal, but a power. For the only thing that can control a power is a stronger power. And in the Christian faith, that power is love. But what is described as love in much of our culture is either sentimental or sexy and therefore not germane to the kind of power Christianity means by the word love. I cannot do justice to this in one last paragraph; it's worth at least another letter.

Meanwhile, I want you to hold me to strict account on this problem of self-interest. It is, I believe, the key problem of morality and ethics. Precisely because I have been critical of other views of self-interest, it is my responsibility to deal more adequately with it. And this I hope to do next time in a "positive and enlightened" way. Aspirins anyone?

Yours for basic surgery, etc.

— 5 —

MR. JAMES NASON
ELM STREET
OLD CITY, COLORADO

Dear Mr. Nason:

I understand your brother is out of the country on a business trip. I promised him a second letter and since I too will be away shortly I wanted to write before I left. Therefore I am addressing it to you and trust you will see that he gets this upon his return. Since Paul said that my first letter was discussed with you, I also trust you may be interested in reading this letter and corresponding too, if you wish.

The problem at hand is the relation between self-interest and love. As I said in my last letter, too many people think that Christianity is against all self-interest and wants it replaced by pure love and service of others. It is essential therefore to point out that the Bible calls for no such thing. It is obvious that we cannot get rid of the self and its interests. The problem is to control and direct the powers of the self and to determine what are good and bad uses of these powers. In short, what is valid self-interest and what is sinful self-interest?

One of the most concise statements of the Christian view on this problem was given by Bernard of Clairvaux who defined the highest type of love as "Love of self for God's sake." He puts this at the end of a little list which he called the four stages of love. The first level was "Love of self for self's sake." This is obvious egoism. The second stage was "Love of God for self's sake." By this he meant our attempt to make God do what we want him to do. How modern this description is! God is on our side; let's try to manipulate Him, use Him for our desires. Offer a few prayers, pay in some Sunday premiums and then He will pay us off with success, and so on. The third level is "Love of God for God's sake." Now this would seem to be the ideal. But Bernard pointed out that such a love is a kind of absorption into God. The individual loses himself and his individuality and becomes immersed in God. This is not real love because it is one-sided and results in the loss of the self. Therefore, real love is love of self for God's sake. Here then is the affirmation that there is a valid self-love, a necessary self-interest.

We can put this valid self-concern another way. It is the Christian faith that God loves all men. If God loves me then I should love myself. By what right could I hate myself, regard myself as useless and of no worth? God believes I have worth in His sight. Therefore in my own sight, I have worth. Now, this has nothing to do with our moral or immoral status. The Bible assumes that nobody can stand before God with moral purity. "O Lord, if thou shouldst mark our iniquities, who could stand?" Jesus said, "No one is good save the Father." But part of the Good News of the Christian faith is that regardless of how bad we are, God believes we are worth redeeming. The quaint but still widespread belief "Be good and then you'll get to heaven" is denied by the Bible. We are *not* saved by good works; we are saved by forgiving love which is known and received in faith. Thus, the whole point here is that because God loves me I can love myself. I know that no matter how I have failed or boasted, hated or hoped, I am worth something to God and therefore to myself. So we begin then with the affirmation that all men have worth and dignity. We have no right to hate ourselves. We may and often should hate what we have done or not done. But our basic self as an individual person, we should love and respect because God does.

From this basic start, it then follows that we use the self and its powers for God's sake. What does this mean? It means that I have not only a right but a duty to maintain myself, to grow and cultivate whatever abilities have been given to me, to raise a family and provide them with the necessities of life. This is valid self-love and self-interest. This is fairly easy to describe and understand. But, of course, the problem arises immediately when you introduce the obvious fact of other people who have the same right and responsibility. Two family men competing for the same job—what then? And you can enlarge this almost indefinitely: two (three, thousands) competing for the necessities of life, groups vs. groups, nations vs. nations, etc. Let us say, for example, that I win the job position. Naturally I feel fine about this. It is good, it is necessary; nothing wrong about getting a job. This is valid self-interest. But what about my competitor? He lost. Certainly any concept of genuine love means that I have some responsibility towards him. Indeed I had a responsibility long before the job was awarded. For during the competition, what was my relationship with him then? How easy and natural to say almost anything goes, for the sake of my family, you know. But what about his family? And again our inclination is to say that his family is his business, not mine. But this won't do. Such an attitude then leads to a battle of warring egos each trying to justify itself on the moral grounds of valid self-interest and family interest. If this is the only basis, then our morality is clearly a primitive tribal ethic, and we end up in a dog eat dog or group vs. group warfare. To avoid this, God is present. For He reminds us that the nature of love is the concern for the other man and his family. Therefore I cannot run roughshod over another man. On the other hand, love does not mean that I give in and do not compete so that he gets the job. This would be abdication of my love for myself and my family. But it does mean that there are limits to what I will do in the competitive struggle. Love means that I will not double-cross my competitor, nor tear him down by gossip behind his back. It means that I will not descend to bribery and false flattery, even if he does. In any case, the point is that a problem is always raised because of competition. This is the nature of life. I should love myself, I should love my wife, my children, other people, my country, other countries. But there are inevitable conflicts all along the line. How can I love my children equally, especially if one is more demanding than the other? How can I love my neighbor who needs a friend desperately, but who irritates me terribly? How does one love America and the people of Russia when we despise the tyrant? It is obvious, then, isn't it, that there is no simple formula for love and morals.

So we say there is valid self-interest and there is the valid necessity of loving others. But it is terribly complex. This is why we must avoid the beguiling claims of easy answers, sure-fire formulas, facile moral guideposts, and comfortable rationalizations of righteousness. For where does valid self-interest end and required love for my neighbor begin? No matter where I draw the line, I can never be sure it is right. Humility becomes me, therefore, and the need for further help becomes more urgent. This is why I've always liked Woodrow Wilson's rejoinder to the proud man who boasted to Wilson that he was a completely self-made man. To which the President replied, "Well, I'm glad you don't blame anyone else."

Perhaps it would help clarify what we are trying to say about love if we pointed out the difference between loving, liking, and hating. In the Bible, Jesus made this quite clear. He loved the Pharisees, but he did not like them. He hated hypocrisy, sham and evil, but called for forgiveness seventy times seven to the doer. Our first clue to Christian love, then, is its universality. We are commanded to love all men, not some of them, but all of them, for everyone is our neighbor. Frequently, our response to this kind of love is to regard it as an impossible ideal. For we are inclined to say, "How can you love somebody you don't know?" And here we are confusing friendship with love. It is true one cannot be a friend of someone he has never met. But one can love an unknown stranger. What does this mean? Well, it points out the second characteristic of Christian love, namely, its disinterestedness, its objectivity. By this I do not mean that love is *un*interested, nor self-interested. I mean that love is given for its own sake. For example, Christian love cares about what happens to people anywhere. I do not know anybody in Africa, but Christian love impels me to care what happens to people there. Or, I may dislike a neighbor, but love prompts me to try to understand why he is irritable and provocative. And should he get in trouble, love would prompt me to help him. Christian love cares for people as persons; it is concerned about people of all kinds. Christian love has nothing to do with whether you like or dislike a person.

I suspect that many a person has left the Christian faith because he believed that Christian love meant liking all people. And since it is obvious that we don't like everyone, we have concluded that love is impossible and therefore abandoned it. I'll put it bluntly: I do not have to invite into my house every Tom, Dick, and Harry, Jew, Protestant, and Catholic, to prove that I have Christian love. There are some Jews who irritate me; there are some Catholics whom I dislike, and there are many Protestants who either bore me or just make me mad. Does this mean I hate Jews, Catholics, or

Protestants? Obviously not. It means that I dislike some people who happen to be of some faith or no faith. I dislike them not because they are Protestants, Catholics, or Jews, or humanists, or atheists, but because of their individual personality and behavior. The point is we have likes and dislikes, always will, but these feelings are not what is meant by love or the lack of it.

If I have Christian love, the likes and dislikes will still be present. It is both futile and dishonest to pretend that we are free from such likes. But Christian love enables one to be concerned about all kinds of people. It enables us to respect their individuality, their rights, and their uniqueness. Christian love suggests that we try to understand why they are that way. It gives us insight and sympathy and imagination to see that if we were brought up the way they were, we would probably be pretty much the same. Indeed, Christian love also suggests that we may have some responsibility in the dislike or animosity. I can be irritable and unreasonable too. And often a cool or indifferent relationship is not a question of liking and disliking, but a difference in interests. My neighbor likes fishing; I like golf. He likes to talk about chemistry; I like to talk about theology. He likes the Yankees, I go for the Red Sox, etc. There is little common ground between us, so we are pleasant to each other, but neutral. But love can abound without cocktail parties.

Christian love, therefore, is universal; it cares about people; it seeks to reconcile. Now reconcile often implies a previous relationship that has been broken. In human relations this means that some fear, egoism, or misunderstanding has been the cause of the rupture. Love seeks to re-consider, re-concile, get back together. But again, reconciliation does not mean you have to invite to dinner somebody you dislike, though in some cases, this might be a way of overcoming the dislike. Reconciliation means re-establishing the relationship on a new basis of love. For instance, in many management-labor disputes, there has been at least a brief history of fairly good relations. There has been some degree of trust, appreciation and mutuality. But one strike may have broken that relationship. Now there is mutual suspicion, hostility, and unfriendliness. The dispute may have been settled economically and financially by an impartial arbitration board. Employees are back to work and the plant is operating full steam, but the relationship between employer and employees is still basically broken. Christian love is what tries to reconcile the two groups again. The president may never like the union leader, but he need not hate him. Both can learn to appreciate the pressures and responsibilities on the other. Both can learn of the self and group interest inevitably present in themselves and their position. Both can begin to reach beyond to the public interest. Both can seek genuine reconciliation.

Finally, what about hatred? I would say that hatred of a person is primarily caused by one's own egoism. I hate somebody because they have hurt me or threaten to harm me. I hate because I fear. I hate because someone stands in the way of what I want or want to be. Of course, there are many other reasons. But essentially hatred is born of egoism. If this is true, then it should be equally obvious that we cannot rid ourselves either of egoism or of hatred. And again, I wonder how many people have abandoned Christianity because they feel that Christian love meant the absence of hatred. And because they knew they could still hate, they believed that therefore they could not love. But the historic Christian faith has never said that we are free from hate. Like egoism the problem is the control of it. Hence the Bible says that we are "to hate the evil and do the good." Here is the key point. Transfer our hatred of people to hatred of the evil. An ancient Christian prayer sums it up best, "O God, give us an abiding hatred of the evil we oppose, and a generous forgiveness to the doer of it."

Again look closely at Christ. It is clear that he hated the evil done to people—the stoning of the prostitute, the indifference of the authorities to the plight of the poor. It is clear he did not like some of the Scribes and Pharisees. It is clear that he loved everyone, for he wept over the fate of *all* the people of Jerusalem. "O Jerusalem, Jerusalem." He understood the Pharisees and the prostitute, Pilate and Judas. He liked some, disliked others, was neutral towards some (like Pilate), he hated evil, yet he loved even Judas and Barabbas.

So my plea in this letter is not to confuse loving, liking and hating, but to see their difference and their proper use. And also to see that Christian love is not the absence of self-interest but controls its proper use. Of course much more could be said about love, liking, and self-interest. But I trust this is enough for now, especially since it is a little on the theoretical and abstract side.

Dis- and self-interestedly yours, etc.

— 6 —

Mr. Robert Crandal
Peerless Steel Co.
Peerless, Illinois

Dear Mr. Crandal:

It must seem pretentious for me to advise you on labor-management problems. Since I am an outsider, you might ask quite properly what business I have in your business, and how could I even know what are your problems. But this letter is not advice, and because of my ignorance of your situation, I do not pretend to pontificate with answers. My primary interest is to try to apply Christian love to a concrete set of problems such as management-union relations. Thus, what I would like to do is to make a try in application and then have your criticisms and evaluation. I am trusting you, therefore, to tell me frankly whether you believe the application makes any sense and has any practical value.

First, let's get a few obvious but necessary points out of the way. I assume, for instance, that we both agree that management and unions are here to stay, that the government will always be a factor in our economy and power relationships, and that military needs will comprise a sizeable portion of our national production for the foreseeable future. If we can agree on these assumptions, then we do not have to waste time arguing about theoretical and "iffy" issues of what it would be like if there were no unions, no government interference in the market and no appreciable defense spending. That unions, government and hardware constitute very complex problems goes without saying, but that they are now part of our life is equally obvious.

We can assume then that our concern is how to apply Christian love to labor-management relations. My first suggestion would be to say that the first need and act of love is honest and rigorous self-analysis, self-criticism. I say this because I believe this is the first act of love and because I believe that in recent years both management and labor have done very little of this, at least publicly. Both sides have fired many broadsides at the other with the usual result of defensive reactions and hardening of the negotiation arteries. For example, labor usually takes a look at a company's profits and then accuses the firm of narrow self-interest, greed, and stubbornness. Management, in return, calls attention to a few notorious racketeers and/or the wage improvement over the last fifteen years and accuses the union of narrow self-interest, greed and stubbornness. There are other variations of accusations and rationalizations. But the result is the same. The lines are drawn, the negotiations long, tempers increased, relations deteriorated, and often a settlement is reached only by external pressures either economic or governmental. But nothing is really settled; it is only postponed until next year. Can this dreary round of bitter conflicts be lessened?

Would it be possible for a given company or union to take the initiative and dare to be a little self-critical? It is probably asking too much to do this in public, but that some serious self-analysis be done in private seems to me to be essential. But of course, the chief problem in self-analysis is the degree to which we are able to be honest with ourselves. In an individual, but particularly in a group of like committed people, it is often very difficult to be objective. For we are all partly prisoners of our group thinking and culture. It is not that we are consciously dishonest or even lack the will to be fair. Frequently, our sources of information and attitudes are one-sided. I very much doubt, for example, if many union leaders read *The U.S. News and World Report*, *Forbes*, and *Barron's*. Similarly, I suspect few management executives read union newspapers, *The Democratic Digest* and the writings of Robert Nathan. Much self group-analysis, therefore, goes around in its own circles and too easily puts the blame on the other group. Probably the best example of this fact is to compare the arguments between the company economist and the union economist. Frequently, both men use the same set of economic facts and statistics but come to opposite conclusions. This proves that economics is not a science and that both economists are partly captives of their employers.

If there is some measure of truth in the above observations, then it would seem essential that some new procedure for group and economic analysis be established. I am wondering, therefore, whether it would be possible for management and union officials, and economists, to meet regularly and exchange views and information, to share common problems, and to work out possible longer-range plans and programs. As an outsider, I could not specify the exact structure and procedure of such a plan. And what is the right form for one company may not be the correct way for another. Each group would have to devise its own procedures and methods. But I am convinced that much more could be done along these lines than is now occurring.

There are, of course, many difficulties involved. One is the sacred cow of management's right to all policy making. Basic policy decisions are still regarded as the sole prerogative of the executive. The second problem is the sacred cow of the unions' drive for more power and security. There are other barriers, but I believe in most cases, these two cows are the chief road-blocks to management-union joint consultation. Now, I am not asking that the two cows be destroyed; I am only suggesting that they be regarded as regular barriers, not holy untouchables. This cutting down to proper use and size could be done by several methods—and you could think of many more, I am sure. For instance, let management cut out the public relations nonsense that *all* the stockholders of a company own and run it. While it is partly true that stockholders who own huge blocks of stock *may* have some influence on company policy, the vast thousands of people who own five or twenty-five shares have nothing to say about policy, and most would not want to if asked. The management executives and directors make policy, period. Let us not flatter falsely the separate little stockholders. On the other hand, let us face the fact that company policy is *not* made purely by management. It is also made by external pressures from the union, the government, the international situation, and the real or imagined public opinion. But the key point here is, of course, responsibility. Regardless of pressures, internal or external, management is responsible for the policies it makes. And this is where the union difficulty arises. Several companies have tried to bring in union officials. The union has often welcomed the opportunity of sitting in on the councils of management, but when asked to assume responsibility for their part in policy decisions, the union has almost always balked. Too many want power without responsibility. Union representatives are afraid that if they agree with a certain policy not in accord with some extreme union demand, then the rank and file will regard their representatives as "selling out to the company." So it seems obvious that the unions have a job of self-reform too.

At present, the unions bleat about responsibility, but it is almost always a lecture to management on their obligation to the consumer. The unions need to do something about their responsibility to their company. But if the company does not invite them in to policy deliberations, the union cannot get very far. On the other hand, if management does encourage participation, but the union refuses to accept responsibility, then the whole procedure is futile. And so the dreary circle of charges and countercharges continues. So what to do? I agree that at the present time there are some companies and some union officials who are incapable of joint consultation. But I am equally convinced that there are some firms and some union leaders who are capable of such a program. I am saying that in such instances a break-through in relationships is possible. It is worth a try, many tries. If some of the larger industries and unions really set out to achieve this, I believe some significant improvements would happen. Failure has been due to the sacred cows on both sides, and the feebleness of the attempts, plus the fear that one side might lose something. Well, where is the spirit of your many Chamber of Commerce advertising claims about the entrepreneur who fearlessly takes risks, welcomes adventure, and breaks new grounds for progress? And to the union we say, where is the spirit of your self-advertised image that you are not racketeers and self-interested men, but giants of service, public responsibility, and cooperation? I suggest it is time for a little honest pioneer work in human relation from both sides.

This call for consultation this far is fairly obvious. If you agree with me and such attempts were made, it seems to me that some of the basic issues which must be dealt with are of key importance. Here is our sacred cow again. And I would like your specific comments. For instance, *should* management have the *sole* responsibility for determining policy? Since company decisions affect the livelihood of thousands of employees, should *they*, the employees, have *some* voice in determining such policies?

I would think that they should. The management argument that the company takes all the risks and therefore should run its own firm without interference from union, government, or the public is not true most of the time. For a small company the possibility of bankruptcy is greater. But when G.M., U.S. Steel, or similar companies use this argument, it has a hollow ring. Bankruptcy is not a daily anxiety for them. But for labor, the anxiety and real threat of lay-offs is a frequent concern. And clearly one of the historic reasons for the rise of unions was to offer some protection, some voice, and some compensation for employees. Great as the power of the contemporary union is, the average employee is still subject to the uncertainty of a livelihood, something the average executive does not face. Therefore, it seems to me that employees should have some voice in the making of policy decisions.

One of the great mistakes of some companies is to imagine that labor will be happy if their wages are adequate. Union bargaining amounts to a representative voice in wage level policy decisions. But by and large it is a fight, not an amicable settlement. And, as we all know, the union culture seems to require its leaders to press for higher demands every year. If the union official does not increase the gravy, he is regarded as an inept failure. This pressure forces him to make both outrageous demands and ridiculous pretensions of moral welfare for his men, the public, the country, and the fight against communism and what not. It is this culture, as we noted above, which makes it difficult for him to advocate, during a recession, a hold-the-line policy, let alone a small wage reduction. So I am aware that much reform needs to be done in the ranks of labor. Nevertheless, most labor unions want more than a 10¢ raise; they want more voice in other policies which affect not so much their wages, but the problems of production such as seasonal goods, cut-backs, lay-offs, model turn-over and so on.

Granted there is some hesitancy to assume responsibility for any decisions, and granted management can't have a union election on every economic policy, I still believe ways can be found to include union representatives on matters of basic company policy making. And let's not rest content just with the suggestion boxes and a bonus or two.

I guess what I am trying to say in this letter comes down to two things. First, that in the past and too often in the present, both management and labor have treated each other primarily as economic power centers. Management has too often assumed that if you give enough meat to the lions they should be happy. The unions have assumed that management is loaded with power and profits and really don't give a damn about anything else. I am saying that both assumptions are now false (if ever true). The stereotypes linger on but need to be destroyed. The problems and responsibilities and issues both groups face are much more complicated than the images portray. Secondly, in order to get rid of the fake images and proceed towards solving the complex problems of our time, it is essential that *some* group take the daring initiative and try to make a break-through. I have suggested or used the concept of mutual and continuing consultation. I do not know whether that is the right word or even the right structure. But you know what I mean, and you know that only by trial and error could a valuable structure and process be worked out. But that it could be done, I have no doubt.

In closing, let me say, not as an argument nor as a threat, but only as a guestimate, that I believe the present management-labor relations are so bad that the government may be forced to create some kind of "Settlement Board." I very much doubt that this would work. Instead of consulting with each other on a continuing basis, both sides would meet only under the pressure of a strike or a government order. This would merely be an extension of the present feuds in the presence of an umpire. The umpire might be able to settle the compromise, but he will never be able to reconcile the contestants. A voluntary arrangement has a much better chance not only to settle an argument, but more important, to establish and maintain better relations, even perhaps to reconcile one group to another.

Voluntary and mutual and regular consultation and sharing, anyone?

Consultingly yours, etc.

— 7 —

MR. GERARD HARRISON
GENERAL AIRCRAFT CORP.
JET CITY, CALIFORNIA

Dear Mr. Harrison:

You write to tell me that you have heard of my suggestion that management and labor should consult more with one another on matters of policy and that you have tried it and it didn't work. You also pointed out that such an endeavor was tried in post-war Germany and it didn't work there either. While in sympathy with the suggestion, you consign it to the realm of another noble but futile ideal.

Let me acknowledge that I probably did not make clear in enough detail what I was shooting for. So let me now try to spell it out a little more. I agree that an ideal picture of several labor leaders or foremen sitting in on company Board meetings and jointly arriving at policy decisions is an unreal portrayal and probably unworkable. This would be a kind of business "summit" meeting without any secondary-level-diplomatic preparation. Actually, what I have in mind is a lower-level area of communication and consultation. For instance, in the area of management relations with the business agents of the unions, there is room for considerable improvement. Many agents have considerable technical knowledge of what is going on in various parts of the shop. Not a few agents can see places of inefficiency and questionable management procedures. Their information and suggestions are often ignored by management, particularly on the junior level. There are many reasons, of course, for such inattention: personal jealousy or fear, suspicion, personality conflicts or misunderstandings. But in addition, it seems to me that another strong cause is the old stereotype problem in which management holds on dogmatically to its absolute right of all policy decisions. Therefore, it resents any interference from labor or any other source. Some executives feel that even if the agent's suggestion is a good one, one should not accept it on principle. The principle being that policy is the right and responsibility of management. Therefore, once you open the door and make an exception, labor will come all the way in and chaos will reign.

When labor is frozen out of any direct influence on company decisions, their only alternative is to effect indirect pressure. This is done, as we all know, by various annual wage demands and/or by slow-downs and pressures through the business agents. And, of course, labor has its burden of a stereotype, namely, that management doesn't give a hoot about labor as people. Executives are only interested in speed-ups, time studies, efficiency, production and profits. Thus, the two stereotypes clash frequently and neither side benefits from this kind of constant warfare.

All I am trying to do is to suggest ways of breaking down the barriers of misunderstanding and hostility. To this you might well reply by saying that such a suggestion is nothing new; it has been going on for years. To which I would reply: True, but not enough. For instance, the old suggestion box method, and the bonus for a new invention or efficient short-cut is still okay, but it doesn't go very far. These methods deal largely with little individual tinkerings here and there, but almost never with any really basic procedure or policy. And anyway, it is still management which evaluates and makes all the decisions and awards.

Another plan of greater proportions is, of course, the share the profits method. Such a plan gives labor a feeling of greater share in the company, greater incentive to produce efficiently. This is all to the good, but from my viewpoint, it is still not good enough.

The profit sharing plan does not really meet the problem of communication between management and labor; it does not really deal with the issues of policy making and mutual understanding. The profit or stock sharing methods or the wage tied to the standard-of-living index are fairly automatic procedures. To be sure, they tend to increase work incentive, reduce the likelihood of strikes, and spread some of the gravy around. But these plans do not deal with labor's complaints against bad management, poor marketing procedures, low specifications on material, arbitrary lay-offs and so forth. And from management's side, these methods do not deal effectively with problems of seniority rights, incompetent foremen, shoddy workmanship, intra-union power struggles, and slow-downs. The point is that the basic assumption behind most labor-management plans is that labor will be happy as long as they get enough of the gravy, whether it be in the form of higher wages, fringe benefits or stock shares. It is this assumption that I am challenging. I believe that most people are never satisfied with any level of wages alone. The worker sometimes thinks that if he had a wage level amounting to $10,000 a year, he would be satisfied. But I would argue that unless the *non*-economic parts of his job were satisfactory he would not be content. If he liked his work, his boss, his foreman, felt that management was efficient and respected him, he would tend to like his job and his salary. But if he regards the job as just a means to an end, a living, then he will make endless demands.

I call your attention to this problem on the executive level. Management is never really content with a little more of the gravy. For instance, look at the executive fund in some large corporations such as Bethlehem Steel. The top executives receive salaries of $50,000 up to $300,000. One would think that such an annual stipend would be more than adequate. Yet, an Incentive Fund is produced by taking a percentage of the annual profits of the Corporation and then dividing it up among only the top management. In most cases, the Fund gives to each individual a bonus equal to or greater than his salary. Thus, an executive whose salary is $100,000 may well receive $100,000 or $125,000 more. I do not say this is wrong by itself. But when some stockholders questioned whether the Fund should be operative in war-time and whether it should be that high, management defended the Fund and the percentage on the grounds that "without such incentive, management could not continue to do their proper job." Point: how much incentive do we need? If I were a steel worker at $6,000 per year, I would not feel greedy asking for $500 more per year; incentive you know! And where do you draw the line?

Thus, it seems clear to me that we are dealing too much with economic man only. I am saying that we can never really satisfy man no matter how much economic goods he has. I would agree, for instance, that even though you ask the ditch-digger and jackhammer worker what he wants, he will reply "more dough." Consciously this may be partly true. But whether he knows it or not, he wants more than money. All men want more "things," but they also want meaning in their life, in their job. They want to feel a part of a group, they want friends, they want to be treated as persons, they want to feel worthwhile. A higher wage, better vacation policy, better lighting, music, a good cafeteria, etc., at best can be considered as symbols of management's concern for labor as people. At worst, such methods can be interpreted as attempts to keep the animals quiet, to buy off protests. My point is that with new and fresh attempts at communication and dialogue, the best interpretation and response will be felt. I am saying that now is the time to try new methods and new plans. So the "summit" plan failed. Well, other ideas will fail too, but not all of them. So let's try and keep trying various methods, and see which ones will work out. I suggested a closer consultation between the business agents and the junior management. There is nothing automatic or magic about this plan. One would have to do some preliminary spade work with both agents and executives. There will be some poorly equipped agents and fearful, irresponsive executives. But with a little effort, the best on each side can be discovered. Legitimate areas for discussion would have to be agreed upon and some limits to policy decisions defined. And there would be some issues upon which no agreement could be reached. But, let's not abandon the whole venture; let's go on in areas where agreement can be made.

Let me be more specific. Here are some issues which might be considered in such labor-management meetings: (1) Problems of automation: will a new super drill-press-assembly machine put forty-two men out of work or not? If so, can any of these men operate the machine? And if five could, what of the other thirty-seven? Is there something else they can do in the shop? If not, will the company tide them over and help them to get another job elsewhere? (2) What about the incompetent foreman, the inefficient tool man, the tyrannical superintendent? Is management helpless to interfere here? Does the union have some responsibility here in spite of seniority? (3) How is the demand for a speed-up related to the company's competitive situation? Is it speed-up or perish?

Is there a danger of lowering of quality? (4) How can seasonal lay-offs be eliminated or reduced without slow-downs and without sudden company announcements? (5) A host of other problems which you, in a company, could spell out better than I.

Now it may be that working through the business agent is not the most effective approach. In one plant, the top union leader may be the best man, the one most knowledgeable and understandable. In another plant, the union leader may be an incompetent loud-mouth, while the foreman may be the best avenue. In some companies, the vice-president level may have the most adequate persons. You see the point. The basic principle here is the obvious ethical one of understanding and mutual appreciation and reconciliation between labor and management. There is no one right plan of achieving it. It will never be achieved perfectly. Each company will have to experiment and find out which method is best for its situation. There will be failures and some modest successes if both sides keep at it.

One final point: I have the feeling that my promise at the start of this letter to be more specific may not have been fulfilled in your eyes. I came up with no detailed blueprint for a management-labor solution. But I am sure that we would agree by now that there is no "*the* solution." Nevertheless, I believe I have raised some sample problems, have argued that these problems can be dealt with by some type of specific arrangement, and that such plans will have to be worked out on a trial and error basis. Indeed, many companies are doing precisely that. I guess the real emphasis of this letter is to stress the urgency of further endeavors, the willingness to try harder, and especially, the imagination and courage to be more daring. But behind even these fairly obvious suggestions are a couple of less obvious but more basic issues, namely the assumptions under which most people have been operating. I have suggested, for example, that too often we have been treating each other as if we were only economic animals. That we have strong economic drives and needs is beyond debate. But that we have non-economic drives and wants should also be obvious.

Many corporations have recognized man's psychological needs and have hired various kinds of sociologists and psychologists. Some of these psychological methods and policies have done some good. But here again there is an assumption which needs to be challenged. For the majority of psychological analyses and methods tend to treat people purely in terms of stimulus-response animals. Hence the soft-music background, the right tints and colors in wash rooms and lunch rooms, various word symbols to be used in hiring and firing (one is not "demoted" but "transferred")—these and a host of other methods have their proper use and place. But basically they will fail because they too cannot be a substitute for the deeper aspects of human nature. For example, if I believe the company is producing a low quality condenser with a short life, soft music and good food will not make me take care and give precise attention in making the condenser. Or if the foreman is a tyrant, a green formica lunch counter will not solve that problem.

Again, let me try to make this clear. I agree that a bright table top is better than a dirty brown one, music better than the harsh grind of a lathe. But is it not also true that man has other even more basic needs? What needs? I hesitate to use the word "spiritual" because it is so often over-used and perhaps misused. But I think you know what I mean by this word. I mean man's desire for meaning in life, for significance and worth in his job, his desire to be treated as a person rather than a thing or a unit, or a number; his chance to have some say and some responsibility in the decisions which affect his livelihood and so on. My emphasis, therefore, on communication, consultation and dialogue, and sharing, is a way of achieving these profound needs. The emphasis on urgency and imagination in seeking new concrete ways of realizing these aspects is due to my belief that at this point in labor-management history, we are in a crisis.

While there is some progress in the destruction of stereotypes, there is a long way to go. But more important is the power struggle. Both management and labor now have enormous power. I suppose, over-all, one could say that the power is now about even. There are variations; some unions may be a little more powerful than the company; this would be particularly true in a small company. In other instances, G.M. is probably still more powerful than the CIO. But in the long view, considering the almost unlimited power of industry in the Robber Baron Age, the present power situation is about even, with the government now acting as a possible third power rival. The point is that labor-management relations are now largely a power contest in which neither side wants an even draw, and both sides would prefer a victory. The steel strike of 1960 was a pretty clear example of both sides trying to gain a power victory over the other. It is my view that if this kind of struggle continues, it will do no one any good. Neither side can win, only the public will lose, and this, in turn, will cause the government to intervene to the satisfaction also of no one.

Thus, it is time to take steps to eliminate the armed and hostile truces and seek reconciliation. This cannot be done by propaganda releases to the public. The basic first step is establishing communication between management and labor. Then both sides can begin to talk and to share common concerns. This does not mean that management has to give up managing. It means that both sides can learn something from each other, but more important, deal with each other as human beings with common concerns, diversities of gifts and joint responsibilities. I think it is time to spend more time on human relations, and I would call this the most practical necessity for labor and management.

May I have a communication from you on this?

Relatedly yours, etc.

— 8 —

MR. ARTHUR POLLARD
VICE PRESIDENT, ALLIED MOTORS
MOTORVILLE, MICHIGAN

Dear Mr. Pollard:

Your discerning criticisms of the several books dealing with "the organization man" and the life of management executives is certainly worth a response. And I agree that, at many points, the pictures and arguments are overdrawn and overemphasized. But, of course, it won't do to ignore the basic criticism just because some parts of it are exaggerated. Thus, I should like to have your comments on some of the following observations.

It would seem obvious that in any group activity, some kind of "team spirit" is essential. There is no quarrel, therefore, with the general idea of creating an organization spirit, a group ethos, an organization attitude. I suspect the legitimate area of debate is the kind of attitude and spirit engendered and the methods used in achieving it. For instance, I believe you would join me in rejecting any organization which, in the interests of efficiency, required conformity on all matters all down the line. This would be an extreme example of the tyrannical top brass creating a bunch of yes-men underneath. On the other hand, an opposite extreme of a full plant discussion and vote on all matters up the line would be just plain chaos. So the obvious solution would seem to be somewhere in the middle. But just saying we are middle-of-the-roaders and leaving it at that, won't do. One reason for spelling it out is that there are good and bad mixtures of a middle ground. For example, some organizations have the appearance of a nice mixture of freedom and responsibility, but in fact, they are largely paternal. That is, the boss may not be an obvious crude dictator, but what he says "goes," and let no one dispute him. In addition, there is usually a pretty clear pecking order, and if you want to get ahead, you play the game, or else.

For another reason, the very nature of any group tends towards conformity. This is true not because any one person or group of people is especially evil or power mad. It really is in the nature of things. It is always easier, for example, to continue policies which have been in practice for some time. It is always easier to give orders through established channels and expect to have them carried out. It is always easier and quicker to have an executive make a decision without having to take the time to consult, to discuss, to argue and finally to arrive at decisions by a majority vote. The efficient and fast use of power and authority almost always seems to be the best way to get things done. Again, I would argue that this phenomenon is not peculiar to the business world, but is equally true of all organizations including the Church. My point is, then, that there is a natural built-in tendency for all organizations to drift towards centralized power, conformity, tradition, autocracy and bureaucracy. In order to resist or control this drift, it takes continual and conscious action to maintain a proper balance. Are there, then, any guidelines and principles by which we can define and maintain a relatively good middle ground position? I believe there are, and so here is an attempt to describe some of them.

First let us take the problem of power. There is little doubt, I think, that highly centralized power seems to be the most tempting and efficient way to get things done. But on deeper analysis and by many empirical examples, I believe it can be proved that "it ain't necessarily so." The only assumption for the efficient use of power by an authoritarian is that the user is wise enough and virtuous enough not to misuse power. Lord Acton's familiar dictum that "power tends to corrupt and absolute power tends to corrupt absolutely" is true. Or in Christian terms, we would say that the doctrine of sin teaches us that no man is wise enough and good enough to be trusted with too much power. Further, in practical examples, one can show where the power wielder did make mistakes. The history of many businesses is filled with executives of considerable power who may have started off fairly well, but who eventually made technical mistakes, short-sighted judgments, wrong guesses, or in their later years, became power drunk, or traditional in methods, or crotchety, or just senile. But whatever age or experience level one looks at, it seems a fact of human nature that nobody should be entrusted with too much power. No one is wise enough and good enough to be our lord and master unchecked.

Therefore, the basic issue of power in any company is how shall the use of power be distributed, checked and balanced? Here again, it is obvious that there is no Christian blueprint or any other perfect plan. Here again, we can say that we are against monolithic power structures on the one hand, but on the other hand, we are against too broad a diversification of power so that everybody has a little, but so little a part, that no one can really make a decision and no one is really responsible. Here again, we end up in the cliché that we are middle-of-the-roaders without having said anything important. Yet knowing what to avoid is a necessary first step.

The next step of trying to define a healthy, viable, and efficient middle position is, of course, the most difficult. And again we would agree, I am sure, that there is no one right structure of power. The small business organization will differ from the large corporation. And significant experiments are being tried. For example, General Electric's dispersal into five relatively independent production groups several years ago was an attempt to curb a monolithic tendency, as well as seeking a more efficient means of production and use of managerial talent. Other corporations are beginning to devise various systems of critique, executive sharing of ideas. And not a few business leaders have said that they are crying for imaginative and competent people, that the chief problem is not so much the structure of the organization, but the lack of top flight men. This may be true, but I believe one must ask whether many organizations have a structure and an ethos which would encourage and recognize a first rate man. I would argue that such is not always the case. Yet, in terms of most organizational structures in American business today, I believe the power problem is controlled fairly well. Most businessmen believe in the marriage of power and responsibility. Most structures do not have a tyrant at the top. There is a fair amount of the right type of dispersal of authority, checks and balances. There is room for improvement, of course. But on the whole, management is aware of the power problem and is working at it. Wherever there is a bad use of power, more often than not, it is not the structure, but some individual who is misusing his power. All structures and plans can be corrupted by individuals. This is not to say that plans and organizational procedures are useless. They do, in fact, put some limits on individual sins and weaknesses and often establish responsibility. But it is also true that no system can eliminate human sin. Therefore, we must still experiment with better organizational power structures, but we must also go on to the next step, and that is the creation of better cultural attitudes within management and organizational life.

The third step, then, is the image of itself that a company tries to create and maintain. Here I am not describing the public relation picture that is presented to the public. Rather, I am trying to deal with the image the company tries to create for its own management and employees. For example, some firms stress efficiency, procedural order, proper channels of orders, standardized routine to the extreme. Here is an attempt to solve various business operations by external structure and forms. The price of this overemphasis is a tendency to so standardize everything that improvements and changes become both expensive and difficult to initiate. If the market competition requires relatively frequent adjustments and new improvements, a rigid system will tend to respond rather slowly. More important, however, from my viewpoint is the cost in human behavior. The paradox is that a streamlined organizational structure is designed in part to curb individual weaknesses and to achieve efficiency, yet the very same standardization also tends to curb initiative, eliminate imaginative ideas and methods, and make personnel slaves of machines and methods. And, if this occurs, then efficiency in keeping up with the market is reduced.

Or, other companies develop an exaggerated "team" image. While the cooperative attitude is obviously necessary, it can be overdone so as to eliminate effectively valid and genuine controversy and differences of opinion. Too much "togetherness" may often be achieved at the price of conformity. In personal relations an artificial friendliness is the order of the plant, particularly among management personnel. The "keep smiling," the frequent handshake, backslapping, jokes, false compliments, ready agreement on opinions and judgments, etc., all in the image of the big happy family, produce an irritating degree of hypocrisy. This kind of image puts an enormous pressure on individuals to conform to the stereotype.

By contrast, some other firms create the model of the tough, hard headed entrepreneur. Here the attitude is "I can be tougher than you." So the office is filled with yells, shouts, snarls, terse phone calls, insults and threats. Woe to the man who takes such abuse personally; he could not stand it. Instead, he is expected to "play the game," take it in stride, dish it out and produce, or else.

Well, these are some of the obvious extremes, but a more subtle and widespread corporation image is the large "family" or "community" picture. In this method, a company not only tries to create a "one big happy family" spirit in the plant, but also tries to extend it beyond the day's work to the home and community life of its employees. Executives are often urged or expected to join the Rotary Club, the local church, and the Community Chest Fund. Employees are given all sorts of written advice on the desirability of participating in neighborhood projects, how to be more sociable, better educated, etc. And recently, not a few companies have strongly urged political participation. Obviously, all these ideas are not wrong in themselves. But the reasons and motivations behind such participation are indeed open to question. The general theme of much company literature is that one should engage in these activities either to ostensibly better himself, or to further the interests of the company. An analysis of most literature dealing with political participation reveals that the company bias is pretty clear. That the labor political advice is even more biased and more obvious does not excuse either labor or management.

Quite apart from any general or specific suggestions about political action, what I am trying to point out here is that in the above-mentioned procedures some companies are really trying to dominate the whole life of their employees. One can find, for example, specific suggestions of what books to read, what types of recreation and clubs to engage in. This is not to say that I am charging business with the old "company town" mentality when the firm owned all the stores, banks, and houses. To be sure, this kind of economic slavery is happily passing. But what I am charging is that in our time we are seeing a kind of cultural slavery. I would grant that some of this is an unwritten policy, but in some instances, it is carefully planned. And I say it is immoral.

There is no moral reason why an employee, as an employee, should join a church, club or political party; no valid reason why he should read this or that book, participate in The Little League or not. Status in the company should not be determined by whether the employee is playing the company cultural game or not. By what right does a company try to mold the social and philosophical or religious or political values and attitudes of its employees? I recall having visited a firm and walking through a large office filled with some one hundred or more architectural draftsmen. I was appalled to see that all were dressed exactly alike: white shirts (sleeves rolled up a certain way), black ties, dark gray pants. I felt like shouting: "Isn't there just one man who wants or dares to wear a blue shirt, or maybe just a brown tie?"

I am saying, then, that many companies are producing a dangerous image and attitude. It is dangerous because it tends to groove its individuals into a company mold. Morally, this seems to me to be a denial of individual freedom, variety, and initiative. Practically speaking, I would also argue that it is bad economics, and ultimately, bad business. The difficulty is that to encourage variety, and imagination, and the creative maverick, is to make administration procedures more difficult. It is always easier if everybody agrees and everyone can be relied on to do the same thing, to react the same way. To have to deal with variety, the non-conformist, the maverick, always is more upsetting, time consuming, controversial. Let me stress that this is not the peculiar vice of the business world; it is inherent in all groups, all administrative structures. Even so, just because it is difficult is no reason for giving in to the easy out.

My conclusion concerning the problem of the "organization man" is that it is morally and economically essential that a business firm experiment with organizational structures, procedures, and image-making that maintains on the one hand efficient methods of production and sales, and yet on the other hand provides a maximum amount of individual freedom, dissent, controversy and imaginative creation. And the reigning necessary assumption behind such experimentation should be the awareness that all groups tend towards conformity. Therefore, if we must err, let us err on the side of creative freedom. I suspect that the top responsible management really wants this and that the chief stumbling block is among junior executives who believe that they must "play the game or else."

Yours for more mavericks, etc.

— 9 —

MR. JAY HARRISON
GENERAL APPLIANCE CORP.
CHICAGO, ILLINOIS

Dear Mr. Harrison:

You write to say that you have read some Church statements which severely criticize an economic system which is based on the motive for profits, and that the Church authors say that, instead, we should produce from the motive of service. Your criticism of this simple view seems to me very discerning. I would agree that no business can operate purely from a service motivation. If the outfit is going in the red, it cannot operate very long, and the old-fashioned Christian doctrine of sin should have informed the authors that nobody is good enough to act from one hundred percent pure service motives. However, these statements were made during the 1930's by a group of idealists. The main stream of Christian thought does not hold to such a view.

On the other hand, I cannot agree with what seems to me to be your too easy identification of profit with public service. While profits are necessary, there is no automatic relation between a successful business venture and the public interest. I very much doubt, for instance, whether the public interest is better served by another profitable cosmetics or toothpaste firm. The market in these two items is glutted. The public has a variety of choices.

An intensive drive to produce another brand, and at a profit, does not, I submit, contribute a public service. This, of course, is a minor example only. But the issue of profit and public service is a very large and complicated moral problem. And I do not see how it can be solved either by an idealistic appeal to an altruistic motive or by affirming an automatic answer derived from a profit system.

I should like to spell this out a little more precisely because it is often overlooked. For example, when the issue of ethics and business is raised, most of us begin talking about how to be kind to employees, how to develop better human relations inside the business, better relations between labor and management, executives, managers, foremen, workers, etc. And this is a necessary ethical-moral field. Over-all, American businesses in the last fifty years have made great moral advances in this area of human relations. That we have a long way to go is equally obvious. That some businesses tend to substitute psychological manipulation for human relations is also evident. That inter-personal relations is a rather clear moral area is likewise evident. But the whole economic field of manufacture, marketing, pricing and selling has been largely ignored in moral terms.

Most of us believe that basic economic policy decisions are purely economic and have nothing to do with ethics. For example, we might ask: Is there a Christian quota of production? Is there a special Christian way of manufacturing a product? What has ethics to do with competitive bids in a building contract? Are there not purely technical economic questions which are totally unrelated to ethics? Of course, I would readily argree that there is no special Christian way of making steel or packaging goods. There is no moral rule for purchasing raw material. There are many technical economic problems such as depreciation wear in plant machinery, ways of amortizing loans, etc., which are relatively if not completely non-moral problems.

To illustrate my point, however, let me suggest some economic problems which I believe are also moral problems. Is there not a moral limit to the amount of profit? My own answer to this question would affirm the need for a moral limit. On the other hand, I would not think it possible to define specifically what the limit was and then claim that my definition is absolutely morally right. One cannot say that ten percent is *the* moral profit margin for all products, all corporations for all time. A twenty percent profit one year may be necessary to pay off or make up for a previous bad year of deficits. And if a firm only makes four percent profit one year it cannot claim it was morally robbed. Then there are a host of other economic variables such as research, possibilities of expansion, re-tooling, replacement, and so forth. In short, I am agreeing that profit *is* a necessary economic question. But in addition, I am asserting that moral decisions *also* are related to profit. For example, if a firm has a good year and makes an enormous profit, is it not morally obligated to see whether or not it might fairly reduce the price of its products to the consumer? The usual response of most firms in such cases is to declare a better dividend, give out bonus to its employees, and build up its reserves. These policies are not bad per se, but they leave out the public. I am suggesting that the ethical principle of the public interest is a valid moral concern and should be operative when possible.

A second economic-moral problem is the question of the methods of competition. Can we morally afford to say that "anything goes" in the competitive situation? Not a few businessmen have pointed out that "you can't turn the other cheek in the business world" and "only the strong can survive." And quite nostalgically these same men, therefore, conclude that one can't be a Christian and a businessman at the same time. The alternative thus seems to be that "dog eat dog" is the only way to survive. My response to this situation is to agree that perfectionist ideals are not realizable in the business world. But I would quickly add that such ideals are realizable nowhere in the world, including the Church. Surely, it should be obvious by now that almost every moral choice in life is a choice between shades of gray. But, just because we cannot choose a perfectly good path does not mean we have to choose a totally evil one. Indeed, civil laws are there to try to protect us from the obvious evils of fraud, murder, extortion, etc. Surely most businessmen have some idea of moral limits. And yet sensitive men know also the very serious pressures and temptations to cut corners and go beyond their intended limits. For example, a small building contractor who is just barely surviving and, let us say, is having a bad year, will be sorely tempted by an offer of a complementary contract bid. As you can tell from this remark, my moral system says that complementary bids are wrong. They are wrong because they violate the legitimate free market of competition, they deny the client the most efficient and fair price for his building, and they violate the integrity of both contractors. And yet think of all the plausible rationalizations one could give for agreeing to such a deal: "Everybody else does it, why shouldn't I," "I'm doing it for my family; if I don't survive this year, my boy can't go to college," "Until the law stops this sort of thing, I can't change the practice by myself," and the like. All very human and understandable reasons. And I would go further and say that if the contractor gives in and agrees to the arrangement, he is not some special kind of moral devil. But what is essential here, it seems to me, is for him to recognize that if he did agree, he did give in. He did make a moral mistake. To engage in the practice and come out of it with an easy conscience is to compound the immorality with hypocrisy and self-deception. It is easy for an observer like me to pronounce that he should stand firm, maintain his integrity, and refuse the offer. I would hope that he could. But if he failed, all I ask is honest recognition that he did fail morally, and that he take steps to avoid the next temptation. And let none of the rest of us imagine that we can avoid similar temptations and failures in our respective vocations. We are a community of sinners all beset with similar moral difficulties, and all stand in the need of forgiveness and new strength to deal with the next tough moral dilemma. But again the point here is that our contractor friend had an economic decision to make but it was also a moral one. Thus, there are moral dimensions to competitive methods.

Another area of economic-moral dilemmas in the competitive situation is the pressure on the manufacturer to cut corners on quality in order to survive. The wide use of plastics in consumer goods is a case in point. It is clear that the use of plastics is cheaper, in most cases, than steel or aluminum. On the other hand, a high quality, durable plastic is often as expensive, or nearly so, as a metal part. But a less durable, lower grade synthetic is much cheaper to produce. Thus, many parts of appliances, automobiles, toys, etc., are produced with fairly cheap plastic parts. Considerable evidence has been accumulated to show that this cheap use of plastic has cut down the efficiency and wear of the products. Here, I submit, is a real economic-moral dilemma. In a fiercely competitive industry such as the appliance and auto industries, it is economically necessary to figure out means for cutting manufacture costs. The use of plastic parts is one obvious partial solution. But the moral problem is the responsibility of the industry to the consumer. It will not do to tell the public that they are getting a break or a price reduction. What good a lower price if the quality is lower? At the same time, management can always say that if higher quality is expected, higher costs must be accepted. And one cannot survive if he prices himself out of the competitive market. And so the dreary round of inferior goods continues, all in the name of survival.

I do not know of any easy economic or moral answer to good quality, fair price and market survival. But one thing seems to me quite certain, namely, that if we refuse to see any moral problem in this situation, we shall not come up with any answer at all. What is worse, we shall continue to let profit and survival be the *only* criteria and thereby, in effect say, the public be damned. But, of course, no public relations department would ever say that in our time. They would compound the immorality by publishing all sorts of nonsense about the glories of free enterprise competition, how much better off we are than the Russians, how management thinks only of the consumer and what he wants, and on and on. I say it is time for us to come of age morally, to acknowledge that this and similar situations are very complex economic-moral dilemmas, and then begin to struggle with them, agonize about them, and try to do something about them.

I hope you will not regard this letter as a pious call to be a Boy Scout in a man's world of complexity, or regard this as a lecture to an insensitive businessman. Quite the contrary, I hope I am able to appreciate in some small way what terrific problems you face. Further, I know that many men are wrestling seriously with some of these moral dilemmas. And surely the celebrated anti-trust cases of 1961 against the major electrical companies high-lighted the existence of such economic-moral problems. The real tragedy of that case, to me, was not that there was a coordinated price rigging deal, but that the top executives disclaimed any knowledge and all responsibility for the policies of the defendants. It is inconceivable to me that such major policies of such large proportions and practiced for so many years could be unknown to the top brass. And if actually unknown, are they not at all responsible for major policy practices within their company? This is not to say that I regard price fixing as acceptable. I should think we would all agree that it is not fair. That there is a tragic hypocrisy involved here too is obvious. For surely, these companies do their part in filling the land with pamphlets about the need for preserving and maintaining free enterprise, free competition, individual initiative and the consequent benefits to the consumer, the nation, democracy, freedom, and the American Way of Life. I take no pride in pointing out the hypocrisy here, for who is more guilty of hypocrisy than a sincere Christian? We fall short of our Lord daily, we do not fulfill our professed ideal of love. So again, those businessmen are not some special brand of sinners as a result of their malpractice. But it must be noted that here was an example of moral feet of clay, of the moral dimension in economic policy decisions, and of the fact that there is no natural or automatic public benefit in business success.

In calling attention to the tragedy of the high brass disclaiming responsibility for the price-fixing policies downstairs, I do not want to seem to minimize the practice of rigged pricing. Surely no one is so naive as to think that only the electrical companies engaged in such practices. I also realize that many competitive prices are fair. But I think we must admit that there has been and is a good deal of "gentleman's agreement" going on in our economy. As to who is actually and specifically guilty of rigged price policies is indeed a matter for the courts. All I am saying is that price agreements are moral as well as economic questions. And I am taking a stand here by saying that such fixing is morally wrong.

At the same time, I would want to be the first to point out that the price-fixing problem is not the only moral issue involved here. For example, it could also be argued that if G.E. could produce turbines at $10–50,000 less than anybody else, they would soon put all competitors out of business. Then they become a monopoly and, ironically, subject to another anti-trust prosecution. One could therefore argue that the price-fixing deals kept a lot of companies in the market, spread business around, thereby helped employment, etc. These latter arguments do not, in my judgment, justify the fixing. But they do point up further the complexity of both the economic and the moral problems. This case showed that there is more than one economic and one moral issue involved. The defendants were nailed on the one moral issue of concerted price fixing. The other moral issue of spreading business fairly and equitably, of avoiding monopoly, was not considered. And doubtless you could mention still other related problems such as, for instance, the scramble of the victims to receive financial redress far beyond the probable just and actual damages. But surely this case was a large example of an economic-moral problem.

Profitably (?) yours, etc.

— 10 —

MR. RAYMOND CARTER
UNITED MOTORS CO.
DETROIT, MICHIGAN

Dear Mr. Carter:

Your frank and forthright letter arrived a couple of days ago. I did not know that you were a close friend of Jay Harrison at General Appliance Corp. in Chicago, but I am glad he felt free to send you my letter to him on some problems of policy decisions and morality in business, and I welcome your forceful observations.

You say that in the auto industry you do consider the public interest in many of your policy decisions and that much of the health of our economy is dependent upon the car industry. Therefore, you reject emphatically the stereotype that auto magnates are grubby, profit-seeking egotists. Instead, you affirm your concern for the public and its needs and wants, as well as your responsibility to the national economy as a whole.

By way of response, let me re-affirm that in my letter to Mr. Harrison, I did not accuse anyone of being the devil! I was trying to describe a few sample problems which pointed up the complex dilemmas of moral decisions. To be sure, I was challenging any notion which claims that there is an automatic relation between profit and public good. "What's good for General Motors is" *not* necessarily or always "good for the country," or vice versa. I should like to explain this further, shortly. But I was also trying to say why there can be no cut and dried moral rules for specific policy decisions. At the same time, I was attacking the idea that the Christian ethic had *no* relation to economic decisions. I believe the auto industry affords a rather clear illustration of the complexity of moral-economic decisions, as well as pointing up the need for relating ethical, indeed theological, principles to the problems. So here is an attempt to do this, and I would appreciate it if you would read this letter and then send it on to Mr. Harrison.

First of all, I would agree that the auto industry has a major influence on the national economy. When you have a bad year, you order less steel, less parts, etc. This affects many side industries and suppliers. In addition, you have to have lay-offs. This in turn reduces purchasing power among many thousands of workers. Some might argue that a bad year is really a chicken and egg story, namely, that other factors in the economy cause a low consumer demand which, in turn, causes a bad year for you. I will not try to settle that argument. The only relevant point here is the obvious one, that whatever the original causes may be, when you have a bad year, it does have a deleterious effect on the national economy. And the converse would seem to be true also, a good car year is usually one sign among others of a pretty good year all around.

So what is the significance of this point? For our purposes, we could say, then, that it is essential that the auto industry be kept healthy. But how? The how, I submit, raises some tough and very basic economic-moral questions. For instance, if a good year means the sale of seven million cars, can the public buy seven million every year and perhaps gradually eight million? And if the public *can* buy, *ought* it to buy that many every year? I raise the "ought" question because in the late 1950's, various charges of planned obsolescence were made, criticisms of model changes every year raised, and the car manufacturers responded slightly by emphasizing longer new-car and parts warranties. I do not want to get into the specific charges and countercharges of that argument here. A more basic issue seems to me to be the question of production for public need and its relation to profit, and the economic and moral health of all parties concerned. I should hope you would agree at the outset that any simple statement that cars are simply designed and produced in simple response to public demand is a vast oversimplification, and in some instances, just not true. For certainly, advertising and design and promotional campaigns are at least partly designed to *create* a demand. Such efforts are not purely a response to consumer needs or wants. There is, therefore, a moral question as to how far and by what methods an industry should or should not create a demand or a desire, especially if it is a desire for an unnecessary luxury.

A simple moralist might render a verdict that the creation of a desire for a needless luxury is just all wrong. But the manufacturer might quite properly reply that in our economy, unless an industry grows it will die, and that making goods more attractive, appealing to a modest desire for creature comforts, is essential in a competitive situation, and lastly, it is not the prerogative of the producer to legislate aesthetic tastes. Similarly, it can be argued, no major industry can produce only on the basis of some level of Puritan or Spartan need. One can argue that some car models had too much chrome. But is it immoral to offer an abundance of chrome? The customer can always choose another model or another make. And if enough people don't want the stuff, the manufacturer will soon know about it, and respond with less trim in next year's model. So what is all the moral fuss about?

For myself, I would tend to reject both of the above positions, but would probably be nearer the manufacturer's argument, as stated. My position would assert that there is a question of moral responsibility for an industry as to how far, by what methods, and with what degree of intensity, one creates sales demands. Obviously, the ideal would be to stress superior quality. But this won't work by itself. If a really durable car with really durable parts were made, it would last quite a while, and therefore the need for seven or eight million cars per year would be lessened. In order to do both, some manufacturers have been selling the idea of the need for a second car. The moral question here is "Do people really need a second car?" An obvious answer is that some do. But equally obvious is the answer that many do not. Does a manufacturer have the right to barrage the public and bulldoze some of them into wanting the second car? Much of the advertising for the second car plays upon the ego-status of the consumer, arouses his luxury desires, encourages the show-off and "the keeping up with the Joneses." And often an advertisement clearly, and I must say frankly, invites him to be a social snob. I say there is a moral problem here. It seems to me irresponsible to reply that one is only responding to what is in human nature, that one is only satisfying what the public desires even if they aren't always conscious of it. This attitude seems to be affirming a morally neutral position by claiming to make no moral judgments either way. I should point out that such apparent neutrality is not really true, however. For not to make a moral judgment often means either cowardice or acquiescence in evil. An extreme illustration would be to say that if a man robs a bank, why should I sit in judgment and say it is wrong? That is the job of the moralist, the preacher, and the civil judge. This view is just morally irresponsible; it is not neutral. It is the abandonment of morality in the name of objectivity.

On the other hand, I believe I can appreciate the enormous economic pressures on the manufacturers. In our present economic system, one must produce and sell and grow gradually, or one may well go under. A large business, even if it does not go bankrupt but has a bad year, may contribute to a national recession. And one can argue that there is a moral problem here too. For in a slump, workers are laid off, people suffer hardship, more taxes are needed for relief and "priming the pump," etc. Yet in order to avoid one moral evil, is it morally right to engage in another immoral practice? I would argue that it is immoral to play upon the public's egoistic and snobbish desires. I would argue that it is immoral to tell the public that unless they have a television in every room they are behind the times or low on the social scale.

Now let's see what the result of my view might be. It could be pointed out that if a corporation abandoned the immoral creation of needless wants their over-all production and competitive position would decline. I would agree, therefore, that for me to say "your practice is wrong, don't do it, period" would also be morally irresponsible. It becomes the critic to suggest an alternative. An alternative suggestion, clearly not new, is diversification of products. And you in the auto industry can reply to me by saying you are already engaged in diversification. You produce tanks, missile parts, appliances, etc. And I would have to say, weakly, that you should continue to enlarge such programs. I acknowledge the weakness of this answer. But it also leads to an even more basic and broader problem, namely, the whole nature of our economic system, automation, research, the nature of the free market in a technical age and so on. And to pursue this would require a whole book or two on general economic theory and practice which, clearly, I am not competent to write. So the most I can do here is to point out that we have a lot of very tough economic, moral, and theoretical problems to wrestle with. In short, you may quite properly say that I have given one moral judgment on one policy in car manufacture and then come up with a vague retreat into the whole range of economics. And I accept such an indictment. But I would also ask you to accept three of *my* indictments. First, any view that auto manufacturing and selling is purely an economic question and does not involve any moral concerns is just not true. Second, any assertion that any given economic or advertising policy is morally good and pure is also not true. Third, when either you or I make a moral judgment that this or that policy is right or wrong, we have not solved the issue, because one policy is inevitably related to many others. The simple abandonment, therefore, of one relatively obvious immoral practice may lead to another immoral result. Or vice versa, the adoption of a relatively good practice such as fringe benefits for labor, may result in the need for cheapening the quality of the product or raising the price of it. So it should be clear, I hope, that we are rejecting any simple list of right and wrongs as if each rule could be applied unrelated to all the other aspects of economics. But we are also rejecting the idea that because everything is so complicated, no morality is applicable at all.

What then is the answer? To which I would reply with another question, Is there any *one* answer to any economic problem? Clearly there is not. Take any economic problem you want: farm problems, uniform and steady industrial and/or national growth. Both the economist and the entrepreneur have to struggle with a vast complexity of economic dilemmas. But only the coward gives up. So, in the moral area, just because ethics and morality are equally complex, we should not give up so easily.

I should like to close this letter by raising some further issues which I believe to be in this economic-moral category; problems about which all of us should be concerned. Automation is a continual economic problem in our time. And I get a little irritated when I read the casual explanation often seen in company reports to the effect that automation means increased efficiency, more goods, lower prices, and more jobs for men to man the machines. Little, if anything, is said about the unemployment of the workers who have been replaced by the new machines except that there is a period of "temporary transition." I do not believe we are entitled to phrase away the great difficulties involved here. I am not against automation; I am against the too easy justification of it and the consequent inattention to some of its victims. Surely, there is a moral responsibility to help those who are in "temporary transition," i.e., out of work.

Already, technology, among other things, has tended to reduce the work week from sixty hours to forty hours per week. And there is considerable talk of a thirty-five and thirty hour week. This has its possibilities and problems both good and bad. I am raising the question now that if we were also concerned about production for need, would this tend to reduce the production-consumption level? But would that be necessarily bad economically or morally? Our consumption is voracious. The amount of throw-away goods, bottles, cans, parts, utensils, etc., is increasing. Can we continue and indeed increase this use of resources indefinitely? In the long run, economically speaking, can we afford this conspicuous waste of basic materials? In the short run, morally speaking, is it right to produce such huge end amounts of trash and garbage? In terms of our own inner integrity, is it right to sate and glut every desire and fancy? In terms of our relations to the rest of humanity, is it right to consume an over-abundance while millions grub for bare existence?

I raise these questions to point out a similar difficulty in my position. I seem to call here for less waste and do so on moral grounds. Yet I know that to cut down conspicuous consumption would also involve possible further unemployment. In your situation, you call for more efficiency via automation. In my situation, I call for more attention to moral responsibility and fulfilling of needs via less waste. But in both situations, our policies would create more unemployment. The point is, therefore, that one cannot decide such issues in isolation. Both seem desirable, yet both have serious effects on people. So, both of us need to look farther afield and work out the implications of our desired policies. Here then are two situations in which economics and moral concerns are inevitably intertwined.

We seem to be willing to "make adjustments" for the "progress of automation" knowing that it does produce some difficult economic and labor problems. But I am wondering if we are equally prepared to make some moral "adjustments." I suspect that we are not so ready. We can excuse the lack of moral courage by again taking refuge in the cliché that economics is not the domain of morality, that economics runs by its own natural laws. Therefore, leave the market alone and everything will work out all right naturally. This is really irresponsible. Or we may take refuge in the wistful thought that while morality ought to have a place, alas, it is too impractical and too difficult and so it wouldn't work. This, I submit, is the response of the coward.

Again, there are no magic rules or easy moral formulas. And I acknowledge that if we really worked at a concept of public interest, put a little more emphasis on production for need, better and more durable quality, such policies might indeed require some economic "adjustments," compensation for a slower rise in productive levels, wider diversifications, different tax structures, etc. All very tough problems, but whoever really thought that anything important could be easily solved?

Lastly, it should be obvious that these difficult issues will not be solved by ministers like me handing down moral ditties to you the businessman. The moral-economic issues are so knotty that a knowledge of economics and business is essential. I don't have this; you do. But a knowledge of theology and morals is also necessary. I have some of this; and you have some, I a bit more perhaps. This means obviously the need of working together.

Expectantly yours, etc.

— 11 —

Dear Mr. Carter:

In your reply you say that I have really mixed you up by using terms such as theology, ethics and morality without ever really defining them. Indeed, you go on to say that I seem to use them interchangeably and without ever making clear what I mean by such words. And finally, you say that you do not really see how they are applicable to economic and business problems.

I must confess that I do stand at least partly guilty. So let me, in this letter, try to make amends by clarifying my position.

First, let's take the word "theology." For me, of course, that means Christian theology. Theology is a set of affirmations about basic realities like God, the nature of man, values, the meaning of life. Theology is a set of descriptions about what we believe to be most real, most true, most important. Thus, in the history of the Church, there are a lot of formal theological writings. But one need not have written abstract technical books to have basic attitudes towards problems. What, for instance, does the Christian doctrine of sin mean? It means, among other things, our belief that man is inclined towards selfishness and pride. In most issues in life, man's first thought is usually "what's in it for me and mine?" As the theologians say, that is "inordinate self-interest, sin." Man's pride takes many forms: overestimating our virtue or abilities, regarding other people as less virtuous than we are, believing that we do not really need other people's help, and affirming our self-sufficiency so that we do not seek or feel we need God. There are many other examples of sin. But our point here is that Christianity says that pride and inordinate self-interest are the basic causes of most conflicts, hostilities, and difficulties in life. If one takes the doctrine of sin as true and takes it seriously, then it radically affects one's outlook on certain problems. For instance, in an earlier letter, I said that no one should be entrusted with too much power. Why? Because we believe a man's pride and self-interest will inevitably lead him to the misuse of that power.

By contrast, if one has a very optimistic view of human nature and regards man as mostly rational and virtuous, then one could give power to a person without too much worry. You see this portrayal in Plato's *Republic*. His ideal Philosopher-King is regarded as both wise and good, and therefore, Plato gives him near absolute power. Most Christians would not draw such a picture precisely because of the fact of sin. It is our doctrine of sin which tells us: watch out for power in business, in government, in the Church—everywhere. Here, we believe, is a practical application of a theological doctrine.

Further applications of this doctrine tell me the following truths: (1) I will tend to assume that while most of my competitors are acting from pretty clear self-interest, I am acting from more noble motives of family and service, but this assumption is wrong. (2) I should become aware of the myriad ways and temptations toward self-deception about my motives and attitudes. My ready and facile rationalizations should come under the most critical scrutiny. (3) The real choices in life are nearly always choices between shades of gray, and since my motives in selecting one alternative are always mixed too, humility becomes me. (4) And speaking of humility, let us beware of false humility, e.g., taking pride in one's humility; "I'm more humble than you are!" These, then, are just a few sample applications of a doctrine of sin to personal situations. And we could go on to illustrate group sins: group vs. group, an organization's own collective egoism and public irresponsibility. One can often see a fairly high moral level within a group such as the family, a fraternity, a business club, etc., but that same group may be quite ruthless in its attitudes and practices towards other groups, especially rival ones. So we are arguing that sin is not just a matter for theologians, nor is it a simple list of do's and don'ts; it is a basic conviction about human nature. If you believe it is true, your actions and attitudes will be quite different from those of a person who believes in the total goodness of man.

Now, of course, it is customary for many people to think that Christians believe only in the sin of man. This is clearly not true, for we also believe in the essential worth of each individual. Since all men are children of God, and since we believe God loves and seeks all men's redemption, all men have some worth and dignity. Here then is another theological doctrine. What are some of its implications? I have criticized the practice of some firms which try to use psychological manipulations of its employees. I also criticized a view of man which regarded us as predominantly economically motivated. Those who believe this try to solve labor problems by offering more economic gravy, and then wonder why, after a wage hike, the "animals" aren't happy and satisfied.

The Christian doctrine of man affirms that man has psychological and economic needs and wants, but denies that this is the whole story of human nature. We affirm that each individual has worth, and so he should not be pushed around or cast aside like a worn-out machine. We affirm that man's most basic need is to love and to be loved. Incidentally, where does this idea come from? It comes from the Christian conviction that the very nature of ultimate reality (God) has, among other attributes, love. In and through Jesus the Christ, God disclosed that his will and nature was Love. It is the real nature of Reality and our nature to love and to be loved. This is the will of God for man; this is the most basic purpose of existence, the meaning of life. From this it follows, for example, that we are not content with rational arbitration of labor-management disputes; we want to go further and try to eliminate the hostility and suspicion. We want to try to reconcile the two groups. Further, love tells us we have a responsibility to all people, the public, and therefore we cannot stop with satisfying our employees and stockholders. Love also impels us not to fleece our consumers, nor defraud our competitors. And so we could go on and on. But what are we doing here? We are describing and applying a theological view of God, Reality and man. We are saying that basic attitudes towards basic problems very definitely determine how one will act. Let me sharpen the issue by a contrast.

If I believe that all men are basically selfish, that there is no God, that all values are relative, and everybody is out to get all he can for himself by any method he can get away with, then I will go out and try to get my pile. I will be limited only by what I think is a threat of retaliation or loss, or jail. If I can lie, rob, cheat, defraud and fleece people in subtle and undetected ways, why shouldn't I? Why should I seek reconciliation or justice as long as I'm getting my interests served and not hurting too many people too much? I submit this is only a sophisticated version of the law of the jungle, the law of the fang and the claw. But the point is that it is derived from a basic view of human nature, and the nature of life, a view which I believe to be wrong.

Theology, then, does make a difference. What is a man's view about human nature, God, the purpose of life? These beliefs are a man's religion, his theology. What then is ethics? Ethics is concerned with general principles such as: justice, love, righteousness, equality, integrity, goodness. Thus, formal ethical writings try to define and describe what is justice, what constitutes goodness, righteousness, etc. Or one could say that ethics is the general principles which deal primarily with desirable or right human behavior, or better, with the norms of conduct. For example, we are dealing with ethics when we say that "justice is rendering each man his proper due." By this we mean that there ought to be some equality of treatment among all men, that there should be no favoritism. Hence the symbol of the goddess of justice with her eyes blindfolded, a symbol that justice should be administered without fear or favor to all persons. Thus, ethics is concerned with a general symbol or general problem of justice, or goodness, or equality.

It is important to note here, however, that ethics and theology are not separate and unrelated. It is a common cliché in our culture that theology or religion really doesn't matter, only ethics matters. It is often said, "It isn't what a man believes that counts; it's what he does." Of course, what a man does is important. But what he does is largely determined by what he believes, what his values are, what motives, habits and attitudes are present. As we noticed above, if I believe all men are saints, I will act and treat them in a certain way. If I believe all men are skunks, I will treat them in an opposite way. Furthermore, in deciding what is justice and goodness, I am driven back to my basic theological or religious beliefs. For example, if I believe that most men are ignorant, stupid, selfish and only want security, then my idea of justice, power and authority will probably be tyrannical and aristocratic. I would believe in an ethic of the strong and the smart; equality of treatment would be foolish. In this instance, my ethic is derived from my theology. My point is, then, that while there is a difference between ethics and theology, it is a difference of levels, and an ethic is derived from one's basic theological convictions.

We now come to the question of morality. I would say that morality deals with the specific applications of ethics. Or one could say that morality is applied ethics. For example, let us take the general ethical principle of justice. Let us next say we are faced with a concrete and specific question of whether it is right or not to pay equal wages to the same lathe operators at the same bench for the same number of hours and units produced. In order to decide this question we shall first use some concepts of justice and equality. Then we apply it to the specific problem in the shop. We may decide that the application is fairly simple and therefore come up with a decision to pay the same wages. On the other hand, we may also note that one operator is an apprentice, new to the job, a few others are really experts and have been there for some time. Thus, we may decide that length of service, skill and experience should be counted in too. With those additional concerns, we may then decide that a wage differential is more just. Now here is the point: when we define and explain why the experienced senior is paid more than the novice, we are giving a moral explanation and we may be defining a moral law or policy. And we are saying that the decision to pay such and such is a moral decision.

It should be noted here that while there is a difference between morality and ethics, it is also true that they are inseparably related. In order to make a moral decision, one has to use and apply ethical principles. In the example above, it is obvious that the ethical principles of justice and equality were used. But we also used other values such as experience, service, and ability. Thus, we could define the difference and similarity this way: Ethics deals with general principles; morality with specific values. To extend this further, we could then say that theology is concerned with ultimate and basic truths about God, man and history; ethics with general principles of right attitudes and behavior, and morality with specific values and concrete actions.

My chief point is to emphasize again that in any given action we take, theology, ethics and morality are always involved. Of course, I do not mean that when we choose lobster instead of steak, Bach instead of Beethoven, these three elements are involved. Clearly, there are a host of actions in life which do not involve theology, ethics, and morality, e.g., tying shoe laces, drinking water, adding up figures, analyzing chemicals, etc. And there are some actions where it may properly be debated whether they are technical or moral. Yet, whenever a moral decision is made, such a decision also involves one's ethical and theological convictions. This is why I have used the terms ethics and morality interchangeably. I would admit that a careful distinction perhaps should be made in each instance. But I am afraid this would get us into a lot of debatable hair-splitting. Therefore, I am taking the risk that you will overlook some lack of technical precision in favor of what I hope is greater clarity. Again in my own thinking, morality and ethics are part and parcel of the same process. For in dealing with any specific moral problem, I have to use ethical and theological beliefs and principles. And if I were to deal only with ethics, I believe I would be describing only formal and abstract definitions. And for my money, an abstract definition is fairly useless and irrelevant until it is applied to a concrete situation. Thus, one can argue about general definitions of justice and love and not get very far. It is only when we apply or give concrete illustrations and examples of love and justice that the terms assume some meaning and clarity.

In conclusion, I would suggest that the relation of theology, ethics, and morality is similar to the relation of policy, management and production in business. You have basic general policies, goals and purposes in executive decisions, general principles of management and operations, and finally, the specific ways and methods of manufacturing the goods. Each of the three have their own unique and special function, yet each is intricately related and influential on the other two areas, and all three are essential for the enterprise as a whole. So with theology, ethics and morality: each and all together are essential for the enterprise of living, all kinds of living—business, economic, political, family—the whole of life.

May I have your reply?

Morally and therefore ethically
and theologically yours, etc.

— 12 —

Mr. Randall Creighton
Management Consultants, Inc.
New York City

Dear Mr. Creighton:

Your letter raises so many good questions and important observations that only a book could do justice to all the issues involved. This letter acknowledges, in advance, that I am responding only to the highlights of your comments. This letter, therefore, is only a kind of miniature Dr. Spock on The Care, Feeding, and Training of Management!

I appreciate your assertions that management has come a long way in human relations. You say that the old idea of trying to produce a super-efficient machine called a manager is passé or at least passing. You point out that the various training courses deal not only with technical problems, but also psychological issues of adjustment, deeper satisfactions, etc. Further, you mention some of the broader educational programs designed to go beyond economic questions towards more cultural issues, such as literature, philosophy and politics. Thus, your picture conveys the image of what we, in colleges and universities, call "the well-rounded man." With this ideal image, I have no quarrel.

To your major points, then, I would first comment that most of what you say applies only to the top executives in a few large corporations. Three examples are the executive programs conducted by General Electric, Bell Telephone, and Standard Oil of New Jersey. Again, I agree that in these instances, there is some first-rate education occurring, and the whole idea is one which should increase and be emulated by other firms. But even in these programs there are some questions I should like to raise. For instance, how much is being done on raising the ethical issues in policy making? From my observations, very few such questions are discussed. These programs do deal with bettering human relations within the plant, but ethical and moral issues are limited almost exclusively to interpersonal relations, how to be nice to the employees and to each other, and so on. But I have failed to discover any real awareness of the relation of ethics to policy decisions in economic matters. To be sure, there is an occasional general reference to the public interest. But there is little pursuit in any depth even into this area. I am saying, then, that the next basic step in these programs should be the consideration of ethics and economic policy making.

My second criticism would be that much of the approach to interpersonal relations is largely in psychological terms only. I am not against the enterprise and use of psychology. Obviously, one must use and take account of psychological facts. But I am against one school of psychological theory and practice, and I am against what I would call the misuse of some techniques. To be specific, I am arguing against the tendency to manipulate people by psychological techniques and gimmicks. For instance, look at the careful and calculated use of the Dale Carnegie methods of interpersonal relations. You know the rules of the game: the firm handshake, the pleasant smile, ask about the wife and kiddies, butter up his ego, let him talk, flatter him and then when he's ripe, you can "sell" him, or fire him, or transfer him, or almost anything. There are two difficulties with this approach: One, it will probably work if a man is not familiar with the method, but if he is aware, he can spot you coming in the door and predict what you will say. Two, such an approach reeks of insincerity and manipulation. In many instances, the "victim" will know that you really don't care a hoot about his wife and kids, and that your flattery is false. What kind of a relationship is that?

Or take all the various kinds of gimmicks to avoid controversy, promotion and demotion problems among executives. It is a rare event when a top executive tells the real truth to a junior executive about the performance of the latter. Granted there is an attempt at kindness if the news is bad, nevertheless, the frequent fraud of praising the man and telling him he is doing so well that he is being transferred to another department "more consonant with your great abilities" fools no one. And I suspect the hypocrisy of the treatment is often harder to take than the demotion.

I think it is time to take a rigorously critical look at the theory and methods behind our attempts to improve human relations. Too often the theory assumes man to be a mechanical stimulus-response unit to be manipulated by the experts. Too often the method involves using the person for other ends—e.g., keep him happy so that he will be more reliable, more efficient, more productive and easier to manage. It doesn't take very long for most people to know when they are being used. The trouble is that many executives believe that this is all a necessary part of the game and so they go along with it, not because they like it, but because they think they must. I submit that such methods make human relations worse, not better, because the motivation and purpose behind it is wrong. Sincerity, appreciation and understanding of one's co-workers is not produced by manipulation, techniques, and gimmicks. One cares for people as persons, or one does not. No verbal palaver of soft words can make a friend or establish loyalty and respect. We have a long way to go in achieving better interpersonal relations in business and elsewhere.

So much for the top executives. It is in the area of general management below the top executive level to which I should like to make some comments now. You are more familiar than I with the initial recruitment and training procedures of nascent managers. Since most of this involves purely technical education and experience, I have no quarrel with it. But I am sure you are aware of the problem of the team spirit idea, the promises of advancement and promotion. Some of this is desirable and necessary. But an uncritical over-emphasis here is dangerous. For one thing, if too much stress is put on advancement, a manager may get illusions of grandeur and become an insufferable egotist, or he may be tempted to use immoral means to beat out his rivals, or he may arrive at a level which is ideally suited for his talents and capacities, but being told repeatedly that unless he continues upward, he is a failure, he may indeed agree with this conclusion and then flunk out on the very job for which he is most suited and most able. Clearly, not everybody can be king of the mountain. Therefore, it is essential that management policy also recognize that a given sales manager or procurement manager should remain in that position. Assuming he does a first-rate job, it may be that this is indeed where he belongs. To goad him into becoming a vice-president of sales may be wrong for him and for the company. Of course, it is not easy to determine exactly in which instances a man should stay put or go higher. Nevertheless, it seems to me the attempt should be made, as a policy, rather than assuming that, in order to succeed, everybody should try for the top. This kind of pressure results in many an ulcer and many a misfit, and what is worse, the ruining of an otherwise able and productive lower level manager.

And speaking of pressure, I should like to call your attention to some of the pressures put on managers, pressures which I regard as immoral. I would be interested in knowing what your judgment would be on some of the following illustrations. In many retail firms, especially large chain stores, managers are normally rated by sales figures per month or per six months. Often, this is the sole criterion. It is expected that the sales figure should rise by a specified percentage in each "marking period." The store manager who meets the yardstick is regarded as a good one. He who misses is suspected of failure. Obviously, I am not advocating that sales figures be ignored. But I am asking that other considerations be included. Not all towns are the same; some have a more or less stable population, others have a more mobile consumer pattern. In some cities, the firm's store may be in a prime location, in other places, the old outlet is in a declining business area. Then there are a host of other variable factors such as: a bad weather month in the winter, strikes, illness, competition. Any or all of these factors can make a manager look good or bad above and beyond his competency. If sales figures are the sole criterion, the manager is unfairly evaluated. Furthermore, when sales are the sole pressure, the manager, in turn, has to put equally enormous pressure on his employees. Frequently, he becomes the proverbial slave driver or the master manipulator hounding or beguiling his workers onward and upward or else. Human relations suffer, temptations to cut corners increase, reports are falsified, and jealous rivalries appear. The human equation is forgotten, sales quotas deified, all is done in the name of competitive success.

Another illustration of pressure put on managers are some types of sales methods and procedures. One large national company I know of requires its managers and salesmen to make a certain number of calls per day on clients. In addition, the salesman must sell a certain specified type and amount of advertising display as well as the product. He is also told that in order to do this, he must personally count the stock available in the store at the time. Further, he must make out daily sales reports, attend one evening training course per week, one other evening meeting with the area manager. It is also expected that each day's sales trips be carefully planned the night before. His sales day is supposed to start at 8:00 a.m. and end at 5:00 p.m., later of course, on Friday shopping nights. So runs an average week for an average salesman and sales manager in this company.

In an interview with an area manager who had come up through the process, it was made quite clear that the average salesman and sales manager worked from 8:00 a.m. to 5:00 p.m. on the road, and from 7:00 to 10:00 p.m. every evening, with Saturdays and part of Sundays also consumed, especially when monthly or quarterly reports were due. The interviewee also reported that when the company transferred a man, upward or downward, they would frequently notify him on Friday that he was to begin a new job on Monday in a city four or five hundred miles away. It was expected that the wife would attend to the details of selling the house, moving the furniture and finding a new place to live, new schools for the children, etc. Finally, it should be reported that the salaries on the managerial level, particularly from the area level up, were very high, from $20,000 to $65,000.

You may regard this illustration as an extreme example and atypical of most retail firms. And I have no statistics or Gallup Poll surveys to support it with. But I very much doubt that the above picture is far from the mark. A specific policy such as the short-notice move, might not be widespread, but I suspect that most of the other procedures are fairly standard. But wherever these types of pressures are operative, it seems to me that we have some genuine ethical and moral problems. For instance, it is debatable whether the salesman has a right to barge into a store and take a stock count. I do not think it is even debatable in the above example that the amount of required evening work was detrimental to the man's family responsibilities and concerns. Moreover, the company's sales procedures allowed for no exceptions, no extenuating circumstances, and no opportunity for constructive criticism and suggestions. The interviewee, for example, said that much of the advertising material supplied by the firm was too large, too much and often ineffective. When he (and other managers) tried to point this out to the area manager, they were told that it was none of their business; it was company policy and "do what you are told or get out." This attitude seems to me to be tyrannical.

What then shall we say to these things? Of course, one rejoinder to my charge of tyranny and immorality is the familiar one that the above practices are necessary for survival in a tough, competitive world. And I have heard some businessmen argue that they wish it were not so, that they would prefer to be moral and fair and human, but that such was impossible. And so, ruthless policies and pressures are continued all in the name of survival. Well, my reply to this is that such policies are *not* necessary to survival. But please do not now jump to the conclusion that I can offer another way which is perfectly moral and pure and blameless. There is no such ideal and saintly solution. But there is a morally *better* solution. Less pressures can be effected, less demands for evening work, more two-way communication and criticism. Of course there are all kinds of compromises and fine lines to be drawn.

Of course there is a moral ambiguity between efficiency and humanity. Of course there are a hundred shades of moral grays. But the company that says you can't exist in competition unless you forget morality is the one who thinks in black and white terms, or more accurately, just black. I believe it can be shown that any firm which operates on this basis contributes to the decline of our economic system, our culture, our nation and our morality. To be sure, the firm will probably survive and even prosper. The high salaries will draw enough men to survive the pressures, enough egotists and tyrants to keep the sales increasing. In the process, it will ruin a lot of men, some of the brass will die of early coronary, others will have ulcers, and some will just be tough to live with, and families will suffer. In the long run, such companies will make too many public moral mistakes and get nailed for them, or they will contribute further to the decline of morality and humanity. As was said long ago, "What shall it profit a man (or company) if he (it) gains the whole world ($60,000 or a monopoly) and loses his (its) soul?" So here we are back again where we started. We began by talking about sales figures and end up talking about the quality of life.

What I have tried to suggest is that the care, feeding, and training of management had better begin to include something about the quality of life as well as the quality of goods and management techniques. Do you really think this is too idealistic?

Practically yours, etc.

— 13 —

MR. CHARLES HANSON
PUBLIC RELATIONS, INC.
PHILADELPHIA, PENNSYLVANIA

Dear Mr. Hanson:

Your letter disclaiming much influence on business policy and indeed our culture arrived this morning. And I must say that your humility surprised me! The usual stereotype of a public relations man is that he is the bold, brash and dominating egoist who pounds out the propaganda. It is refreshing, therefore, to see that you belie the stereotype. On the other hand, your modesty, sincere as it is, does not seem to me to be altogether true of most public relations men. By this statement, I do not mean that all "the other guys are the bad guys" and you the rare "good guy." My point is that I believe you wield an influence greater than you suspect, for both ill and good.

Let's first look at the company image which is to be offered to the public. I assume that one major premise of the public relations policy is that it is essential to sell the public a favorable image of the company. Granted that every company tries to sell its product on the basis of its quality, effectiveness, price, etc., is it not also axiomatic that, in addition, the image of the corporation is important too? If this is true, then we are immediately faced with a moral problem. The issue now is, shall public relations tell the truth, or create an image resulting in an impression which is only partly true? In some cases, the image may be a very favorable and pleasant illusion, but almost completely false. For example, some companies have tried to create the illusion that the firm exists only for its stockholders and therefore a sizeable section of the public at large. The image drawn here is that the management is only the devoted servant of the public stockholder, housewife, worker, teacher, small businessman, that profits are at a minimum, that whatever residue is available is returned to all as dividends, and of course to improve the plant, and that management is always trying to better the lot of the employees. In short, the company is a real service outfit dedicated to the good of all and democratically run because it is the voice of the many millions or thousands of stockholders who really run the company.

This picture image is not a caricature; it has appeared in the national magazines and in company advertisements. But this is a false image. It is false because the many little stockholders do *not* have any real voice in the policies of the company. The man who owns ten shares of any large corporation stock is a zero compared to a man who owns five hundred shares. More important, trust funds and other firms who own thousands of shares clearly have the possibilities of some influence and control. But even these large trust and corporation holders almost always go along with management's desires anyway. And finally, to insure executive power, all stockholder votes are so rigged that unreturned votes are inevitably pro votes. For management knows, quite rightly, that the average stockholder does not know the real worth of the situation and the validity of the alternatives, and often he does not care. Yet the illusion of the democratic process is maintained. Notices are sent, ballots set up. But what management wants is printed on each ballot, and if the ballot is not returned, it is counted as cast in favor of management—perhaps an understandable and statistically necessary procedure. But let us not blow it up and call it democracy in action. I say this is a moral problem for public relations.

Is it not equally obvious that most corporations are not democratically run organizations? Employees, especially labor, are not consulted on basic policies. One cannot take a plant vote on every major or minor decision, and I am not arguing that this should be the case. I am simply arguing against any public relations firm which tries to create the image that a corporation is a great example of democracy.

Let us look at other illustrations of a partly false image. One popular slogan is "progress is our most important product." It would appear that no one in his right mind would argue against progress. But of course it all depends on what one means by progress. The assumption behind General Electric's slogan tends to equate more and better goods with progress. I could not argue about the need for better quality of goods. But I think we must question whether more goods can be equated with more progress. A family does not need three toasters, three TV sets. We do not need a new car every two years. To argue that we must buy more goods in order to keep the economy rolling and therefore the country progressive, is not automatically true or good. An endless spiral of consumption raises the moral question of whether we need all the goods, whether we are waxing fat and gluttonous, and whether the distribution of the goods is equitable or not at home and abroad. And one cannot, it seems to me, avoid this moral question by saying that it is our job to produce the goods and not our responsibility to worry about equitable distribution. Or another convenient dodge is to assert that we are only producing in response to public demand. The need for advertising reveals the partial fallacy of this assertion, for it is part of the acknowledged role of advertising to *create* demand. Therefore, a producer does not simply respond to a present demand. So I am saying that the production of goods cannot be simply and automatically equated with progress. We must also ask about what kind of goods are needed, what items are essential and non-essential and what the distribution needs are. These are economic-moral questions which cannot be solved by slogans.

Look at another illustration. U.S. Steel boasts that it seeks to produce "the best possible steel at the lowest posible cost." I think one must say that such a slogan is not the whole story. Surely, the company, in all honesty, should add, "and at the best possible profit." Again, I would not deny the need for and validity of profit, so why not say it? Because to say it in public would tend to create the image that the company was interested in profits, perhaps primarily. Since this seems a rather obviously selfish, immoral image, the opposite image is created, an unselfish one. But nobody is that good and therefore the slogan borders on hypocrisy or self-righteousness. This danger is further underlined by the highly debatable question of steel production. Everyone knows that the steel industry almost never produces at 100 per cent of its capacity, and frequently operates at 50–75 per cent. This would suggest that the industry much prefers to operate at slightly less than the demand in order to keep prices relatively high, rather than operate slightly over demand in order to avoid lower prices. This interpretation, I acknowledge again, is highly debatable. But the steel industry has not clearly and effectively disputed nor disproven the above practice and interpretation. Therefore, the claim of "lowest possible price" is not convincing.

Now before you jump all over me on this steel example, let

me quickly say that even if my charge is true, I know that rectifying it is not easy. I know that one cannot simply decide to produce slightly above demand and then automatically reduce the retail price. There are many other economic problems involved such as how one determines what the demand will be six months from now, how one establishes a viable surplus without a serious glut, and how steel is related to consumer demand for autos, government defense contracts, etc. I agree that one cannot solve a moral problem in isolation. All our moral-economic issues are interrelated and therefore involve many complex and ambiguous decisions all down the line. My point here is that the easy assumption that steel is offering the public "the lowest possible price" is not the whole story.

As a public relations man, it would seem to me that you have a peculiarly difficult moral road to walk. Your job is to portray a company in a favorable light. You are conscious of the many unfavorable and unfair images of business and businessmen. It is right that you should want to correct these false images. It is perfectly proper to try and show the favorable aspects of a firm. The difficult moral dilemma is to decide where true aspects of the company end and the false over-emphasis begins. How difficult it is to avoid creating unwarranted impressions. In telling the "good side" of the company and ending with that, is this fair? And yet, how can a public relations department afford to tell the "bad" or weak side of the company? But to print only one side is still only a half truth. A sensitive man such as you must indeed sweat over these issues. As long as you sweat and try to deal with them, I have only admiration for you. It is the public relations man who sees no moral ambiguity and does no moral sweating with whom I would contend.

Another area of moral responsibility in the field of public relations is the influence you have on our culture at large and therefore upon us all as individuals. The image of the businessman and/or business as the savior of our country is one which needs deflating. Some of this deflating process has already occurred since 1952. You will recall the image of the great "moral crusade," how efficient Republican businessmen were to "clean up the mess in Washington," and how the economy would be set aright, taxes lowered, the debt reduced, and how we would get "more bang for a buck." It did not take long for everyone to discover how complex the issues were, and that the businessman has feet of clay like the rest of us. And I venture to suggest that the New Frontier will not be achieved by the younger generation of efficient Democrats for they too have feet of clay and the problems are still with us.

But apart from the past, it seems to me that the image of the efficient, wise and virtuous businessman is still with us and still needs to be cut down to size. What I want to emphasize here is the failure of many businessmen and their public relations men to see the moral ambiguity present in their vocations and economic decisions. This is the point of the examples in this letter. But you go on to overemphasize that business and its executives are the salvation of our economic problems and therefore of actually all our national problems. I challenge this assumption and this sales pitch. I am arguing that even our economic problems cannot be saved or solved by economics, that they can only be solved by a host of non-economic values and policies involving moral, ethical, cultural and political decisions. I am arguing that the businessman is no better equipped, is no more or less moral than any of the rest of us. I am arguing that just as we parsons and professors need to be criticized, so does the business community. And I hope that in my criticisms you will know that they do not come out of hatred, envy, marxism, or radicalism, but that they come out of love and respect for the business community and an interest in preserving and improving our way of life.

Let me then become a little more specific. Many of the public relations releases from business firms and Chamber of Commerce outfits create the image of the noble entrepreneur who is a man of faith and virtue as well as sufficiency and know-how. The image of the natural law of the free-market is also painted. The impression is presented that the Chamber of Commerce and industry are the preservers of the American Way of Life. By comparison, the idea is also conveyed that anyone who disagrees with this image is socialist, un-American, a radical crack-pot or a dupe of same. Elementary honesty would not dismiss in advance all criticism and relegate it to the un-American category. I am sure you would join me in asserting that to reject contrary criticism per se is indeed really un-American.

Finally, my last criticism of image making is the nature of the process itself. Why must an image be created at all? Why not an accurate picture? In order to sell goods, must we go on the assumption that an illusion must also be created? What happens to our culture and our lives if we must create "proper atmospheres," "positive image responses," winning smiles on salesmen, and auras of respectability or superiority? Are not such procedures contributing to a kind of pretence, hypocrisy and artificiality? And is there not in this process of image making another kind of manipulation of people? And if we combine the pictures of how to sell goods with the picture of the noble public service corporation who is saving the American Way of Life, what kind of pretence or claim is this? And it will not do to react by pointing out that other groups do the same thing. I know that image making goes on in the academic and professional world. There are those who try to "sell" the Church to the world. Labor unions have their public relations departments too, and the government contributes its full share. So let us not excuse ourselves by pointing out that others do it too. At the moment, I am saying that there are very serious and basic moral issues involved in the process of public relations and image making. And what applies to business also applies to everyone else. So I am not picking on you as some special kind of evil man in a specially evil job. But will you join me in seeing that there are moral issues here, and that it is our individual and collective responsibility to do something about it?

Yours for less images and more truth, etc.

—14—

MR. B. DANIEL PETERS
CENTRAL ADVERTISING AGENCY
MADISON AVENUE, NEW YORK CITY

Dear Mr. Peters:

It was good to hear from you again and I certainly enjoyed our long luncheon together in "Ulcer Gulch"! Your openness and frankness in both your letters and conversations have encouraged me to really let go this time.

If I should begin by a polemical attack on advertising you would not be reading anything new. Various social scientists and journalists have raked you over the coals before. We both agreed last week that some of the criticism is true, some exaggerated, and some offered no constructive alternatives. I also believe your critics overlooked one important point in your favor, namely, that you *do* have a sense of humor. You do not always take yourselves and your slogans as seriously as your critics think you do. The very humor of your own remarks in conference reveals this. I am thinking of the old gags such as "Let's run this up the flag pole and see who salutes it." And if I were with you today, I am sure you could fill me in on the latest inter-office remark.

And yet behind the humor I think you will admit there is a kind of cynicism which is frightening. I am thinking of the widespread attitude that the primary job of the ad man is to sell the product, that his job is to provide the right slogan, the catchy phrase, the bouncy tune. The ad man himself may believe that a given jingle is really bad, or this phrase nauseatingly sentimental. But if he believes it will sell the goods, he will use it. I am also saying that there is a degrading cynicism in the conscious attempt to manipulate people into responding to the product. The advertising man can quite easily argue that it is not his job to evaluate people's needs and desires. His only job is to sell. So why not appeal to snobbishness, why not use the sex motif, why not encourage the idea of superiority, of status? More of this later. My point here is to note the cynicism of many an ad man, cynicism about his media, about people, about methods. Such an attitude leads to moral decay because it ignores any concept of responsibility, integrity, and ethical concern.

Also behind the humor are the enormous pressures in advertising. All vocations in life have pressures, but advertising has its own peculiar set: shorter deadlines for layout and copy, the frequent need for change, the fear of failure, the consequent loss of a client, and the fierce competition from other agencies. The demand on the individual "idea man" is very great as is the competition between them. To come up with a brilliant slogan or layout every week is impossible. Therefore, the individual lives under the constant fear of failure, fear that he will be "dry," that his rival's suggestion will win approval. The jockeying for power, the envies, the jealousies, the undercuttings, are intense. These pressures are the producers of the ulcers. And the apparently gay, humorous chit-chat of the office is often the artificial veneer which hides the grim conflicts. It seems to me that there is a moral problem in these interpersonal relationships. The primary issue, I believe, is that of personal integrity. And it becomes an issue in several ways. First, how frank and honest can one be in this competitive situation? Can one really feel free to state his opinions in the group, or does he feel required to say what the boss wants, or wait and see what the majority decide and then chime in? Does everyone feel that they must play the facile word game and join the sophisticated cynicism? Or conversely, must one adopt the role of the tough, hardheaded executive, ruthless in his comments, brutal in his demands—the office tyrant? What then about the problem of individual integrity; can a man be himself in such a highly competitive situation? I should be interested in your answers to this. And I suspect your reply will be in the nature of a compromise, namely, that you do draw lines, you do have to give in here and there, and that it is a constant struggle between individual integrity and group conformity. This struggle is not unique to advertising, of course, but I believe it is especially intense there, and not a few men succumb to the pressures and so lose their souls and gain their ulcers. It is therefore a moral issue.

The second problem of integrity is the social side. And here integrity is wedded to the moral issue of social responsibility and public interest. This is the area of the truth or not of the advertising claims for the product. Our recent history is filled with public examples of misrepresentation, some so bad that the government had to step in with a cease and desist order. For instance, the toothpaste ad inferring that "a protective shield" is provided for a whole day was finally banned. The perennial arguments between the mild pain relievers of aspirins with frills were partly phony, one claiming more rapid dissolvement, another claiming nerve relaxation, tension calming, etc. These and other examples are the obvious ones and so patently untrue that legal action was taken. But what about the less obvious instances? What about the whole ethical and moral issue of truthtelling?

I know you agree that there is a very difficult but very real moral problem in advertising. It would be relatively simple if all advertising were merely a job of describing the product accurately. But clearly this is not the case. It would be an ideal but dull dream world if only exact accounts of goods were portrayed. I venture to say that the whole business of advertising would probably collapse. If competitors gave only truthful accounts of the quality and nature of their goods, could they sell them? In our day, is there any real difference between most toasters, steam irons, between Ford, Chevy and Plymouth? Granted there are some minor style and frill differences, can one seriously argue that any one of the three cars is basically superior to the others? Or what has Bayer aspirin got that other aspirins do not have? The answer is nothing, because all aspirin is the same, by law. The net result then is that advertising cannot be conducted purely on the level of claims of quality. Nor can it be successful merely in terms of factual description of the product. At least, these are the assumptions and "givens" of the business in our culture. Therefore, one is immediately forced towards creating illusions and inferences about products. But perhaps those two words are too strong. One could argue, rightly I think, that there is nothing wrong with making advertisements and the goods themselves attractive. Clearly there is nothing immoral about wrapping soap in turquoise or soft yellow paper, rather than dull brown or black. And certainly there is no evil in making colorful and attractive, indeed eye-catching magazine ads. Furthermore, I am a firm believer in good art. One does not always have to have an exact photo or picture of the product. An impressionistic drawing or line sketch may be better. The aesthetic purist would perhaps sneer at the very suggestion of art in advertising. I will not debate that here. I am only noting, in passing, that exact representational styles are not necessarily more truthful nor better art than some other kinds. My chief point then is that there is a valid area in ads beyond mere fact and naked description.

However, I am sure you agree that a large amount of advertising goes well beyond "attractiveness" and color. Advertisements which purposely try to create an illusion, or which definitely involve an intended inference, seem to me to raise a moral and ethical question. One part of the issue is the problem of honesty. Does an illusion mean dishonesty and falsification? Clearly some statements would be lies, as some drug ad statements were so adjudged. But most illusions are not bald lies. For instance, the cosmetic ads most certainly are designed to convey, if not illusions, at least promises and hopes of glamour, irresistible charm, etc. One cannot argue, objectively, that this mascara makes that woman more attractive or not. To paraphrase an ancient cliché: the glamour of mascara is in the eye of the beholder as well as that of the wearer. Or it may be that there is a difference of opinion between the onlooker and the user! However, there is a moral question about creating images, atmospheres, and illusions. And one moral test seems to me to be the question of falsifying the product. This test would also apply to inferences in the text of an ad. Does the inference promise or suggest something which will not happen? The answer to this question can be settled scientifically in drug and food ads. But the problem becomes much more complicated where no scientific test is possible. This brings us to the area of consumer demands, desires, and needs. But to nail down our first point here, I am saying that integrity and honesty introduce the moral question into the use of illusions and inferences.

Related to this moral problem is the second issue about the ethics of appealing to the public psyche. As we noted in the first part of this letter, many ads are specifically designed to play upon people's fears, hopes, sexuality, wants and needs. Illusions and inferences are often designed to evoke or arouse these aspects of human nature. One does not have to think very deeply or look very far to find examples. On newsstands, there are obvious displays of paperback novels with sexy covers. Not infrequently, the picture on the cover has little to do with the content of the book. Then there are mattress ads with naked women aboard, movie ads with lush titles and people, and need we rehearse the cosmetic hoop-la: "Tabu," "My Sin" and all the accompanying phrases, "exotic," "daring," "irresistible." In such examples, it is quite obvious that the ad man is playing upon the sexuality of the public. He is manipulating sex desires in order to sell a product. He is arousing unachievable or false hopes of incredible glamour. Such methods border not only on lying, but on manipulation of private drives for only one end, the fast buck.

In addition, other psychological manifestations are used. Some ads lean heavily on the desire for status and superiority. One must have two cars, or a mink coat, or a Cadillac. One must serve a certain brand of whiskey or else he is a piker. Is it right to encourage people to buy things they do not need? Is it right to entice them into buying things from the motives of sexuality, status-seeking or snobbishness, or fear, or shame? And what about the row over subliminal methods? This seems to me to be a clear case of attempted manipulation of people's desires and wants. I would argue that subliminal advertising presents not only a moral but also an ethical and theological issue. For to engage psychologists in any business firm with the express purpose of overcoming sales resistance and creating a demand, is to violate people's integrity and freedom. It is a kind of brain-washing, differing only in degree from the notorious police state practice. The theory behind this and other manipulative methods is that most people are basically animals, victims of their environment and subject to stimulus-response mechanisms. A few Big Brothers, however, being free from this condition are able to make the sheep do what they want. This is a cynical, deterministic view of human nature, which can lead logically to disaster and decay. Of course, not many businessmen consciously adopt such a view. Most would protest that they believe in the freedom of the individual. Yet the fact remains that when executives use manipulative techniques, they *are* holding a deterministic theory, unwittingly or cynically. And the moral problem arises when someone tries to manipulate people for questionable ends and misuse techniques for private desires. For if manipulation is tried and used successfully in advertising, why not in politics, economics, business, and the whole of culture?

The Christian faith has a different view. We do not deny that man is firmly rooted in nature and greatly influenced by his environment. It is possible to hammer away at people and wield an enormous influence on them. But it is also the Christian view that to assault the senses with such saturation, and to appeal to men's baser drives and desires in order to sell them things they do not need is wrong. We further believe that there are other parts of human nature that are beyond the animal level. There are valid bodily pleasures which should be encouraged and enjoyed: good taste in food, drink, tasteful furnishings, etc. But to manipulate people for any reason is tyranny. This is important to underscore. We are against manipulation for so-called good reasons. It is still wrong to manipulate people to buy Bibles, Christmas presents, flowers or creeds. And it will not do to say that surveys show that the average mentality of the consumer is on a twelve- or fourteen-year-old level. Even if that were true, I would argue that one has a responsibility to raise it, to draw out the best, not to sate the level or degrade it. But again, I would insist that the manipulative methods in advertising are theologically as well as morally wrong because they place a tyrant in command over animals, violate human freedom and integrity, and deny any social responsibility.

Well, these are strong words, but I believe they are fundamentally true and relevant to the advertising business in our time. I think you will agree that the problems will increase rather than diminish. This is likely because of the vast new mass media and instruments of communication. In our electronic age the means of delivering a message are almost unlimited. In short, the power of advertising is enormous. And with power comes the need for greater responsibility and morality. So I close by asking you a question: What's cooking morally in Madison Avenue? If there's nothing on the stove, we are all in trouble and are going hungry.

Yours for a big stew, etc.

— 15 —

Mr. Fred Jarvis
Osgood's Department Store
Middleville, Illinois

Dear Mr. Jarvis:

Your letter raised two basic issues and requested my response. As President of your local Chamber of Commerce, you question some of the criticisms against many prevailing methods of advertising. As sales manager of a department store, you mention some good issues about sales methods.

I shall first try to comment on the advertising problem. You say you agree with my strictures on the more obvious forms of bad advertising and join me in rejecting subliminal and other manipulative methods. However, you insist on the necessity for advertising, and especially the need to create demand. Your point here seems to be that an expanding economy is essential and that one way to achieve this is to create consumer demand. You argue that if demand is not created by advertising, the economy will not expand.

Of course I would agree that an expanding economy is essential and desirable. We can leave it to the experts to determine the exact percentage and rate of expansion. I am not competent to say whether 3¼ or 4½ or 5¹⁄₁₆ per cent is the proper rate. But the real issue, I believe, is the kind of growth, in what areas, and by what methods. Again, I do not feel qualified to delve into technical economic problems, and can only skirt the fringes on some of these matters. What I mean is that I do not believe *all* aspects of the economy must grow. For example, I do not believe it is essential that the cosmetics industry expand and grow. I do not believe we need more brands of toothpaste, soaps, detergents, stockings, neckties, refrigerators, car models, etc. This is not to say that the present manufacturers should not keep up with the expanding population. But it is to say that not all products of the economy are absolutely of the same value or that they need to be produced by more companies. In short, I am raising the old question of production for need again. And please don't give this a Spartan interpretation. I am not arguing that we should produce only for bed-rock basic needs and no more. I would agree that luxury and/or pleasure goods should also be produced. I think it is right that the public should be able to buy a sailboat, a big comfortable chair, the hat with fringe on top, and a car radio. But the decision to make and to buy these goods should be related to a whole vast area of other needs and responsibilities. The automobile industry is a good complicated case in point. A car has become a basic necessity in our life and economy. In the late 1950's the industry had a couple of banner years. The cars got bigger, more expensive and were equipped with more luxury items. The profits were bigger, too. Then came a couple of bad years and a little foreign competition in small cars. Detroit responded with the compacts. These smaller editions successfully squelched the foreign competition. And while the compacts sold pretty well, the profit on them was not as great as on the larger cars. And the sales on the bigger models was still not great. So the manufacturers have begun to heap up the compacts with more extras, more power and more cost, and more profit. Now the tendency is to offer more luxury in the hope of greater sales and return profit. My questions are, do we need this, can we afford it, and is the economy dependent upon this trend? I would argue in the negative on all counts. I would venture to say that what the public needs and really wants is a good car priced at $1,500 or so. There are hopeful signs that Detroit is at least considering this possibility. But there are many objections to it within the industry. It is argued that the profit in such low priced cars would be relatively small. But I would reply that the volume would be enormous. And if someone should point out that the compacts did not sell in outstanding numbers, I would argue that this was due to the fact that they were, after all, priced only a couple of hundred dollars below the little three regular models. And therefore, to offer a car at $1,000 less would really move them.

Now, of course, my suggestion cannot be proved beforehand. Neither could it be disproved. There is always the element of risk. But what is so new about that? The question seems to be whether the auto industry must insist on the steady increase in selling fairly expensive cars at the risk of having a recession and affecting the economy as a whole, or it can go for a low priced, large volume possibility which also meets a very basic need. If my argument has some validity, then it is also applicable to other parts of the economy. Let us continue to have options to buy big cars, big deep freezes, big sofas, but let us begin to produce low cost cars, low cost refrigerators, furniture, appliances. We need expansion in lower cost basic goods in the economy. That such an emphasis would involve some difficult economic adjustments and risks is obvious. But would such a change involve more difficulties than trying to maintain our present policies of luxury and high cost expansion?

Now what has all this to do with advertising? I would say that it has everything to do with it. One of my charges against present advertising is that it does not consider the type of demand it seeks to create. By and large ad men try to create demands by any and all methods. They do not raise the question of kinds of demand, but only react to the demands of the client. Thus, if a client wants to sell mink covered golf tees, the agency does not ask, "Is this tee necessary?" If he is paid, the ad man will try to create a demand for such a tee. I am arguing that it is the responsibility of both the manufacturer and the advertising business to consider production for need—their responsibility to the consumer and to the nation's economy.

It is time for both producer and advertiser to raise some moral questions about their responsibility to the public interest. This means that both need to wrestle with the issues of what kind of product does the public need the most, what adjustments must be made, and what demands should be encouraged, and which should be met but not exploited. Further, the whole relation between the manufacturer and the advertiser needs examination. For does not the producer have some responsibility for the way his product is advertised? And is it not possible for the advertiser to make suggestions to the manufacturer? I am thinking here that with all the vast enterprise of market research, the survey firms have an excellent chance to report public needs to industry. I venture to say that too many surveys are hindsight analyses rather than suggested innovations. To go back to my original illustration, has any research firm ever really conducted an extensive survey on what the public thinks of the prospect of a $1,500 car? And speaking of research analysis, I believe one could raise questions about some of the methods used. How scientific are survey questions and interpretations? Do not some approaches presume a deterministic view of human nature? Are questionnaires designed to deal with subtle nuances of wants and particularly value judgments, or do the analysts get trapped in their own hidden value systems or interpretive categories? Well, this line of pursuit would indeed take us into new fields not within the scope of your questions and my competence.

In summary, then, I am agreeing with you about the necessity of advertising. But I insist that we can no longer afford to create any old set of demands from the public, that it is time to be selective about which needs should receive priority, what tends to serve the public interest, what tends to ignore or debase it. The philosophy of merely responding to what is, reflects moral laziness and ignores the deeper issue of what is healthy or unhealthy, creative or destructive, good or bad. Granted there is no simple way of listing what is good or bad, it is essential that we wrestle with these ambiguous questions.

If the ad men really began to examine the moral implications of some of their pitches, it probably would make the job more difficult. It really would test their imagination and integrity. As with jokes: anybody can tell a dirty one, but it takes a master to keep going with the clean ones.

The second issue in your letter dealt with sales methods. You asked what is wrong with local store advertising and with the quota system on the salesmen. I see no difference here between large advertising agencies and local stores which conduct their own advertising. Problems of integrity, fairness, and on what basis the appeal should be made, are the same for everyone.

With regard to the quota system in salesmanship I would agree that establishing quotas is a necessary and effective method of selling. But can we just leave it at that? Do we not have to go on and raise critical questions about how the system is administered, what flexibility is allowed, and what is the quality of relations between the managers and the salesmen? Are not these questions moral as well as efficiency problems? For instance, what do you tell your salesmen and sales clerks about how to act towards a customer? What is the morality of the hard sell? Does a salesman have the right to blitz and verbally bulldoze a customer into a sale? And are some types of soft sell any better? Maybe some are worse because they are more subtle and really involve manipulation of fears, or of hopes, or false flattery. Granted the difficulties of drawing lines between legitimate soft sell and cruel manipulation, should we abandon the attempt because of the difficulty? Is it moral to say that "anything goes" because that's the way the sales world is, and if you want to survive that's what you have to do? If that is a man's conclusion, then let him be honest enough to admit that his company morality is tucked in a drawer and hauled out only on Sunday, at the Rotary Club on Wednesday, and in occasional public relations releases. The hypocrisy of such procedures is obvious. But the alternative is not to produce silent salesmen, prudish sales clerks and dull displays. The alternative is to do a little moral wrestling, draw some lines on what is advisable or not, and push for integrity and sincerity in methods. I am not so naive as to imagine that quality alone will sell merchandise, nor am I unaware that dirty advertising gimmicks can sell some products. Yet I will take my stand on the proposition that quality and imaginative integrity can sell the goods better.

But now what about the pressures on the sales people? Is it right to demand a certain percentage increase from your salesmen? I would argue that any automatic grading of personnel purely by sales figures is unfair. I would want to know something about a man's methods. I would want to know why X sold less than Y. Were there extenuating circumstances? If so, what kind and how should they be evaluated and compared? If a man does a certain volume of business every year, must we automatically assume that he should increase it? This would be particularly true of salesmen. If I demand ten percent more each year, what does this do to his life, his family, his internal personality? Does the pressure necessitate his working more and more overtime and in the evenings and on weekends? If one man wants to kill himself early by this method, should he be rewarded over the other man who feels a responsibility to himself, his family and his community? It seems obvious to me that these are moral questions facing any sales manager, store executive, and business policy maker.

Of course, what complicates the moral question in the quota system is the fact that it is always easier to administer a procedure automatically. It is much more efficient outwardly to "judge by results," the cold hard figures. To delve into the reasons and circumstances for higher and lower sales, the respective methods of individual salesmen, the extenuating circumstances, etc., involves time, effort, problems of evaluating and interpreting—all very difficult and cumbersome. Thus, all managers and executives are tempted to do what is easiest and apparently the most efficient. They might even agree that it is at least more humane to consider the human equation. But alas, they can also say that they cannot survive in business that way, that figures are clear and the pay-off is not in good-will, but in sales volume. Again I would have to challenge such a position while admitting complexity and difficulty. I would have to affirm, "For what shall it profit a store or a salesman if he gain the whole area and lose his humanity and morality?" What kind of anxious, striving, decadent rat-race is that?

And this leads finally to the problem of interpersonal relations within a store. This, of course, is not a new field nor unexplored.

But I believe it is closely related to pressures, methods and systems used in any company. It is a truism in business circles today that one should be nice to one's employees and fellow workers. Fair wages, fringe benefits, "keep smiling," are all standard practices in most places. So we do not need to go into those things. But I am suggesting that there is a relation between some methods and human relations, that some types of pressure tend to destroy human relations and other methods prevent improvements. It is not enough to speak kindly, smile widely, ask about the wife and kiddies, and then demote a man because of low sales figures. The hypocrisy of saccharine talk and weak rationalizations are all too familiar. "I am terribly sorry, old man, personally I am on your side, but it's the system or the policy or the facts of life, you know. I don't make the rules, I too have to abide by them." This is the type of situation which points up the relation between policies and human relations. To be sure, policies and systems and procedures cannot be avoided. Yet some types of policies may be more humane than others. Therefore, it is the responsibility of the company policy makers to discover which procedures are better than others, not only in terms of sales but in terms of interpersonal relations and well-being. And it should go without saying that every company must keep a weather-eye out for the little tyrant on the make, the arrogant egoist, the clever underhanded competitor who is ready to pull a fast one on his rival and so on. Speaking of procedures, does any given store have a procedure for ferreting out such characters, or does it trust to luck, or does it care at all so long as he sells the goods?

My thought-for-the-week, then is this: that in both advertising and sales methods one cannot separate economic policies from human relations. One cannot say, now here are some ways to be fair to employees, but in promotion and advertising our problem is simply economic and strategic. I am arguing that the specific economic policies adopted may hinder or better human relations, may contribute to the decay or health of the public, and that therefore moral issues are basic everywhere.

Morally and practically yours (?), etc.

— 16 —

Mr. Raymond Ellis
General Electronics Co.
Los Angeles, California

Dear Mr. Ellis:

It is refreshing to receive a letter which is so filled with discerning insights into the thorny problem of government and business. Since I am the barefoot boy in this area, I would like to make some further observations and raise some questions for your comment in another letter at your convenience.

One of the reasons your letter was refreshing to me was your strong criticism of fellow businessmen who lash out against government in business. Large sections of the business community seem to regard most government as evil, even if necessary at times. Various epithets, such as "bureaucracy," "confiscatory taxes," "damned liberals," "greedy politicians," "long-hair do-gooders," "socialism," appear in many executive conversations. In advertisements, company public relations releases, and some Chamber of Commerce publications, there are vast attacks on government in business, and the assumption behind most of the policies is the old nineteenth-century adage: "That government is best which governs least." The cry seems to be a call back to an absolute free market and almost unrestrained free enterprise. But, as you point out, there is something really ironical about all this in view of the fact that so many companies are dependent upon government contracts, directly or indirectly. Your point was illustrated beautifully in a certain town a few years ago. The local Chamber of Commerce and many businessmen flooded the town with various tracts railing against government spending of all kinds, even calling for less defense appropriations. On this latter point, they contended that too much was being spent in fancy research, wild-eyed schemes, impractical theory, etc. At the same time, the town was in bad shape for a variety of reasons, but one chief cause was lack of new industry, with resulting stagnation, insufficient tax revenue and unemployment. Suddenly, the government announced it was going to build a large new plant whose purpose was to experiment with an atomic airplane engine. The multi-million dollar plant was built, 2,500 employees were hired, houses put up, there was more spending and more tax revenue. This plant saved the town. And what was the response of those against government spending? Of course, there was exceeding great joy and the sound of money in the cash registers up and down Main Street. Furthermore, several years later, when there was talk of an economy cut-back in defense spending, it appeared that the atomic plant might be abandoned. At once, the Chamber of Commerce and local businessmen sent telegrams and made phone calls and other appeals to Washington begging the brass to continue the plant operation. As of this date, the plant is still operating and the town surviving. And yet, now that it is a part of their life, there is beginning to appear in conversation and pamphlets the same old stuff about the evils of government in business, the "planners in Washington," and the "crazy theories of the professors."

If I were to end my letter here, it would be likely that a reader would jump to the conclusion that I am a typical liberal welfare stater who believes that the government can solve everything. Fortunately, you know me better than that, and I am not ending this letter here. My first point above is to state my agreement with your observation that many businessmen who howl the loudest against government and politics are dependent upon them for the very success of their business. And this includes many wealthy oil men who have won favorable legislation over the years. At the same time, I would join you, secondly, in affirming the right and necessity of criticizing government at any and all times. Clearly, then, we are saying that dependence does not mean acquiescence, nor partnership the lack of criticism, nor friendship silence.

Equally clearly, I join with you in rejecting doctrinaire notions on the other side, namely, that Washington can do no wrong, that planners are nearly infallible, that only the government can solve the basic problem. In short, you and I obviously reject the dogmas and slogans of both left and right. We would both be in the familiar middle ground position which tries to strike a balance between private enterprise and government participation. But there are at least two difficulties here. One, it seems quite clear that we have a resurgence of the old nineteenth-century dogmas and clichés of individual initiative, freedom of the entrepreneur, courage, guts, survival of the strong and the brave, "shoot first and talk later," personal integrity, and so on. Now no one in his right mind will say that he is against personal integrity, courage, freedom and initiative. But what bothers me is that these virtues are identified and equated with a particular domestic or foreign policy. For example, we are told that the courageous and patriotic thing to do is to pull out of the UN and tell Russia to stop meddling in Asia or else. This is a beguiling and attractive suggestion because it is a simple answer and it is equated with virtue and love of country. It is a devilish suggestion because if one disagrees with it, he is at once regarded as immoral and unpatriotic. Similarly on the domestic front, this group sometimes says that the government should get out of the market and abolish most taxes; that this would then enable us to exhibit our initiative, freedom and courage. Again, this is an apparently simple and highly moral answer, and to question its wisdom is to be called immoral, or socialistic, or un-American. This kind of black and white thinking scares the daylights out of me. It is frightening because it assumes that there are simple answers to complicated problems, and it also assumes that there are simple moral achievements. This is "the good guys versus bad guys" mentality all over again. I had thought that our country was maturing and growing out of this adolescent outlook. I had thought that we had learned something from the puerile black and white dogmatism of the Left. But now, alas, there seems to be a growing imitation of the same outlook from the Right. Thus, I am suggesting that we middle-of-the-roaders face the difficulty of enormous pressure from the Right at home and from the Left abroad. And I am saying that we also face pressure from human nature and human sin. For regardless of labels and politics, it is altogether human to want and to be tempted by simple answers, patriotic slogans, and moral positions. To acknowledge and really know that most of our problems are terribly complex, that our answers are all relative and temporary, that there are many ways to be patriotic, and that our moral posture is always ambiguous and uneasy is the tougher role. And the more complicated and vast our problems become, the more we shall be tempted to adopt an easy out. To put it theologically, I would say that a Christian is not permitted the luxury of an easy conscience or a cliché for an answer. One of his crosses is the agony of complication.

The second difficulty of our middle ground position is that we too must avoid resting in a cliché. Indeed, we are in danger of making the phrase "middle ground" a slogan. It too can be an easy out. It is relatively simple to reject the absolutist and simple-minded claims of the extreme Right and extreme Left. With pride we can say we reject and abhor Communism and Fascism, for we stand in the free middle of democracy. But this won't do either, because the problem is where do we stand? And what is the nature of the middle ground? And anyway, one can't just stand or sit, one must move, one must make decisions and act. So this brings us, at long last, to the basic problem you raise in your letter, namely, what is the middle ground or proper relation between government and business?

Right off I would have to say that any general statement I might make would be relatively meaningless. For example, suppose I adopted one popular stand: "I believe private business should go as far as it can in the economy and then have government handle the rest." This view would include, of course, some necessary referee and police powers against obvious injustices and malpractices. But having said this or anything similar to it, what have I said? Virtually nothing. Such a statement does not tell us how far business can or should go. It does not tell us what "the rest" is. Nor do we have any agreed upon definitions of obvious injustices and malpractices. And what does this statement tell us about defense spending in the economy?

Or suppose, I began with a description of a fairly obvious situation, by saying small business should be relatively free and operate by the free market laws of supply, demand and competition. Such instances would be the drug store, retail appliance and department stores, food markets, barber shops, shoe stores, and the like. On the other hand, state and national highways, post offices, and defense needs are the legitimate domain of government. These two areas are easy to describe and would seem to be clear examples of private enterprise on the one hand and government duty on the other hand. But of course, such a description does not come close to portraying our basic problems. And the defense issue itself brings us right back to our old friend complexity. For obviously, in defense orders there is an inevitable mixture of government planning, foreign policy needs and private enterprise planning, and many other factors. Surely it is obvious that none of us wants to have the government own and operate all industries necessary for military hardware, and no one could maintain the idea that private industry alone should determine military needs, foreign policy and defense planning. Thus, it seems obvious that government and business are here to stay in defense. And surely we need not belabor the obvious point that defense needs constitute a large portion of our economy and affect it for good or ill. Therefore, I do not know of any general statement which can account for the myriad complexities of this problem.

The nearest approach I could offer is still to use the term "middle," chiefly as a sign that I am against the obvious extremes. But then one must go on and show how he lives in the middle. And here I would have to state that my approach is a way rather than a static set of rules. I believe the way is guided by certain basic ethical principles, but these principles have to be applied in each particular situation. And their application will never be exact or perfect. For instance, let us say the government decides on the need for one thousand successors to the Nike-Zeus rockets (let us label the new anti-missile-missiles "Ajax"). I suspect we would both agree that if several companies could make the Ajax, we would be in favor of competitive bids here, and the lowest bid should be awarded the contract. But suppose only one firm can and does make the Ajax, what then? The common practice is the cost-plus arrangement. Problem: is this relatively just? If so, how do we know? Can one say: trust management to determine its profit alone? Or since the government is the client, should it not have some right to examine the books and see if the profit is fair or not? I suspect we would both agree that there is a mutual concern and responsibility of both government and industry here and that one simply cannot use either/or terms. The government alone does not have the right to set the price, nor does industry alone have the right to set the price. Most would agree with the first part of the sentence, but not all with the last part. What, then, is the principle by which I say a company does not have the sole right to determine its price and profit on a defense contract? The principle is concern for the public interest. Defense monies are tax created. A corporation does not have an unlimited right to profit with public money. Therefore the government has a right to share in determining the contract and its conditions and profits. But again, I would agree that there could be no predetermined rigid rules which would apply to all situations. This is why I approve of the review by both sides of any type of cost-plus programs as well as competitive bid contracts. This would be an example of government and business cooperating in mutual responsibility. And I believe such an illustration points up the futility of doctrinaire approaches, yet the relevancy of an ethical principle and its pragmatic application.

Since defense spending is a rather obvious example of the need for business and government working together, we need to raise some questions about this relation in other areas of the economy. And here I would welcome your specific suggestions, for I can only describe in general the situation as I see it. For instance, I believe there is considerable room for legitimate debate about *how much* government control and interference there should be in interstate business such as freight, trucking, chain stores, railroads, etc. Again, I do not see how one could reasonably argue that there should be no government watchdog regulations at all. But it does seem obvious that one could debate the validity and justice of specific policies and laws. Some government regulations, relatively right twenty-five years ago, may be wrong, or unwieldly, or impractical today. Or new conditions may require new policies or laws. Such questions are in the area of legitimate debate and criticism, and doctrinaire positions about no government versus the super-welfare state should be avoided.

Finally, you could list many other areas in equal need of continued evaluation. Just to mention a few: new tax laws, some to stimulate growth in industry, others to plug loopholes; simplified methods and procedures of company reports to government agencies; public utilities under too much or too little government regulation (how does one determine when and where such is the case?). These are difficult enough for any one letter. I look forward to your pearls on these matters.

Yours for muddling in the middle, etc.

— 17 —

MR. HENRY BARNES
ACME TEXTILE CO.
NASHUA, NEW HAMPSHIRE

Dear Mr. Barnes:

You write to ask what I think of the ethics of foreign competition particularly in your type of business, namely, textiles. You also sound off a bit on the government-business problem and request my comments on that issue. I am honored by your request and must also hasten to make clear that I am not qualified to come up with any economic answers to the textile crisis. I thought I'd say this at the beginning of the letter because it will be obvious by the end! Therefore, you will not be reading this under any false hopes.

I should like to deal with your second request first, namely the business-government problem. I enclose a letter on this matter which I wrote to another correspondent, which should give you a general clue as to where I stand. But I would like to continue the discussion with you along some other lines of government-business relations. For instance, I should like to raise the problem of business influence on government policy. This would include not only economic pressures but also political pressures. In this area I believe that economics, politics and ethics are so intertwined that it is almost impossible to deal with any one of them separately. Let me illustrate. Because the textile business is in a desperate situation economically, you are quite naturally tempted to seek some help. Just on the domestic level, the competition from synthetics is enormous. One economic possibility is for a given textile company to go into the manufacturing of synthetics. This is for most firms only a theoretical possibility, for who can compete with DuPont alone? So in most actual instances, a company is tempted to seek government help. Suppose then an economically feasible idea were possible by government action. Would you not feel justified in asking for it? And how would you go about getting aid? I presume you would present your case to the appropriate government agency and/or committee, inform various congressmen who could help put on a little pressure. Perhaps too you would engage professional lobbyists, a public relations firm, put on a campaign and all the rest. Now the question is: what about the morality of your attempt to get government aid?

Let us dispose of a few obvious comments first. One, to seek such government help is not consistent with any extreme doctrine of "keep the government out of business." Second, let us not dress up our request by phony rationalizations to the effect that such procedures are only "expressing our democratic opinion" and "doing our part to make sure we are represented," or "labor influences government, why shouldn't we get ours too?" If we can agree that those two positions are neither honest nor descriptive of the real situation, let us see if we can spell out the basic issues here.

Since I believe in the general principle of mutual cooperation between government and business, I would therefore say that your textile firm has the right to make its plight known to the government. The tough moral questions arise in the methods involved. For example, I have mixed feelings about lobbying. On the one hand, I believe any group has the right to use efficient methods in presenting its case. And a professional lobbyist is often the most efficient system. On the other hand, some methods of some lobbyists are highly questionable. Further, less well-heeled groups and individuals cannot afford such influence. The nearest solution to this inequality might be to put a limit on the amount any firm could spend on professional lobbying. I do not think it is fair for a large corporation to spend $300,000 on a staff in Washington, while the small company can only afford $10,000. Thus, some more equitable limits should be imposed. There are other problems of methods which cannot be solved by regulations, such as the flooding of a congressman's office with literature and letters, the incessant buttonholing at parties, dinners and in the corridors. Misuse of these approaches can only be curbed by client requests, company policy, and individual integrity. Even at best there will be some abuses, and that is why I am uneasy about it. Yet I do not believe lobbying as such is all wrong. It is a way of presenting one's case and often is the most efficient.

My next comment would be to raise the moral question of how much and what kind of pressure should a company put on its own congressman? Granted that you have the right to present your case, will you then demand that he vote for your requests? And if he does not, do you threaten to vote against him in the next election? I would argue that if anyone tries to bind his congressman to an either/or situation, democracy is lessened. Why? Because such a pressure tends to make government *only* a struggle between group and sectional interests. What is omitted is any concept of national and public interest. Now I am not saying that all representatives should ignore the home constituents and always vote for some ideal public interest. Obviously, part of a congressman's job is to represent local interests. I am only asking that we individuals also recognize the national interest (and as I shall argue presently, the international interest). Thus to demand that our senator vote for textile relief or else we will clobber him in the next election, is to ask him to ignore the public interest and other possible valid needs elsewhere. It is the government's job to look at the big picture, to assess priorities on needs and costs, balance the many conflicting demands, and arrive at some equitable compromise and balance.

I realize that I am asking a great deal here. When one is in an economic crisis, it is almost impossible to think of the national interest and other people's demands. Furthermore, one is aware that other larger groups are exerting enormous pressure and influence. Labor's record here is well known and not very encouraging. Therefore, it is quite human to pitch in and see that we get our needs met. Yet one cannot put all the blame on labor either. For various sections of the business world have put vast pressure on government. The most obvious cases are the oil and gas interests, the silver states, and the farm groups. It is understandable, therefore, why a relatively weakened industry such as textiles should try to exert all the influence possible. So I am not picking on you as specially guilty, nor expecting you to suddenly become saints. But I am saying that all of us need to consider the public interest more than we have. To fail to do this is to reduce government to a bitter struggle between competing interests in which the strong and the wealthy will win. This is neither political nor economic democracy.

Another observation which might help us to achieve a better balance between self and public interest as well as to improve business and government relations, is to abolish the stereotypes on both sides. Many businessmen regard politicians as self-seeking little men out for all they can get. And not a few government people will return the compliment by picturing businessmen as fat cats seeking to get fatter at the public's expense. One does not have to be a moral giant to know that there are black sheep everywhere, and it should not take much wisdom to know the fallacy and injustice of all stereotypes. Thus, common decency would seem to suggest that it is time to understand each other with more justice and charity. It is time for businessmen to discover the enormous problems any responsible congressman faces: the endless demands from his own constituents, many of them exceedingly picayune, the vast complexities of national problems upon which he is expected to be informed and to act, the balancing of pressing needs, and so on. And not a few of the pressures are exerted by businessmen, not only valid requests in economic areas, but also the enticing offers of special privileges and favors, entertainment, and propaganda. In the more glaring instances of bribes, mink coats, deep freezes, royal tours and vacations, only the receivers are nailed. Very little publicity is given to the donors. But why shouldn't the giver be equally guilty with the receiver? So there is evil in Washington?—of course! But the job of government is terrifically difficult, and the responsible public servant has an incredibly difficult job. It is time we began to appreciate the nature of his vocation and stop using this word politician as an epithet. Maybe we should revive the old word "statesman" and some of the dignity it connotes.

Similarly, it is time some government people and the rest of us stop sneering at businessmen. For while you have your black sheeps, many men have very difficult and complex jobs. And not a few wrestle with the problem of public responsibility. I am only mentioning a fact, often overlooked, that many people in government and business have much in common, could work more closely together and avoid many of the conflicts which arise from the stereotype mentality.

Finally, let me now get to your first point about the ethics of foreign competition. I believe the moral issues here are fundamentally the same as those of domestic competition. For example, I think we must ask ourselves how seriously we will take our belief in free enterprise and the free market in the world scene. The history of our country (and other nations) has pretty clearly demonstrated that we do *not* believe in a world-wide free competition. Whenever any company begins to lose out in competition, domestic or foreign, it calls for protection. An obvious domestic illustration is the butter maker's successful legal curbs on oleomargarine. An obvious foreign example is your textile manufacturer's demand for tariff curbs on imported wool. The usual arguments for justifying protective tariffs are that we can't compete with the slave wages of foreign countries, and we don't want to put Americans out of work. There is some moral force in both arguments. But it is necessary to point out the fallacy of deciding a complicated issue merely on doctrines of free enterprise. If we stay only on that level, then we must admit that we do *not* believe in free enterprise whole hog. We should be honest enough to say that we believe in it only when we are succeeding and only if all other things are equal (which they never are!). And we should recognize that our arguments about wages and unemployment introduce other relevant problems. Therefore, slogans won't solve the issue and the question is not free enterprise versus socialism, but what kind of mixture of government and business is most desirable and efficient.

I cannot go into all the economic issues of foreign competition, but I can, I believe, mention some of the basic economic-moral problems involved. One does have a moral responsibility to his own employees. But let us not overplay that argument to the neglect of admitting our own self-interest in our own executive and personal survival. In addition, there is the moral problem of our relation to other countries, to other people. From a Christian point of view, we cannot say that only Americans are our concern. This would be only a tribal morality. We are not some special favorites of God, and the rest of the world does not exist to serve us. I am not saying that we are to ignore ourselves and only serve others. I *am* saying that our moral responsibility is to ourselves *and* to all men. That we cannot help all men equally is obvious. But it does not excuse us from doing what we can. Suppose X country is beginning to sell in the U.S. a good quality radio or wool cloth at half the price of our same quality goods. Our natural reaction is to cry for a protective tariff. While this seems to give us immediate protection, it weakens the economy of X which is often a struggling smaller country. Denied sales in the U.S., X may seek it elsewhere, in neutral or Communist coutries. X may even suffer a recession. Then the U.S. may have to bail her out, at considerable cost. Yet, these consequences seem so far away, and "iffy" and vague and general—something for Washington to worry about. In the long run, they do affect us, but in the short run they do not, so we go ahead and call for protection. But this is short-sighted and morally irresponsible. What is the alternative? One possibility would be to have our government require that the price of the foreign goods be raised nearer to our level with the proviso that the resulting increased profits go *not* to the stockholders, but towards raising the level of wages in X. This idea (incidentally, it was suggested by Walter Reuther—surprised? suspicious?!) would tend to make international competition more fair, really test our belief in free competition, raise the standard of living elsewhere, and still be fair to our own industry. Of course, such a plan would not be easy to implement and negotiate, nor would it be successful overnight. I suspect there would be a good deal of trial and error involved. And in the process, some inequities would have to be dealt with.

But I believe it is the kind of imaginative and responsible thinking that is needed in our time, rather than taking refuge in the quick and easy solution of temporary protection that causes trouble in the long run and is morally questionable. It could also be another instance of the fruitful partnership of business and government.

Fraternally yours, etc.

— 18 —

Mr. Halford West
International Manufacturing Associates
Washington, D.C.

Dear Mr. West:

We have argued now for some time on the various ethical and moral issues in business. In your last letter, you express some irritation at my frequent phrases such as: "given the situation," or "within the system," "compromise," "ambiguous mixture," "shades of gray," etc. You quite rightly point out that I offer no clarion call to clear moral actions, offer no clear-cut guide through the maze of difficult choices, and end up each example with a tentative mixture of good and bad. Then you ask whether this is all that Christianity can offer. These comments seem to me to be very basic and so I shall try to respond to them.

Let me begin by agreeing that in most examples and problems examined, I assumed the "givenness" of many controlling factors. For instance, I sometimes assumed without question the economic process of competition, the need for profit, executive and management policy-making, quota systems in selling and so forth. Only within these processes did I apply the Christian ethic. And when I did, you are quite right in saying that each moral settlement was ambiguous and mixed. But is there any other possibility? Is it not still true that if we accept the need for profit the next question is profit for whom? And when we begin to answer that, we are at once forced into considering our various responsibilities: maintaining and improving the plant, providing for research, paying executives and management, declaring dividends to stockholders, and, finally, keeping the public interest in mind. At any moment, we may discover a conflict between our responsibility to the stockholders and research outlays, or between wages of workers and a raise for management. I do not see how one could even expect that there would be a perfect and wholly right solution to any of these questions. So I use the words compromise or balance as a way of indicating that our moral decisions (and economic decisions) always have to consider the whole picture of conflicting needs and claims. Surely, you would agree, for instance, that in dealing with a demand for higher wages, no company can settle such an issue purely by itself. There is no eternal principle of "a just wage" as if it could be clearly applied in isolation. Obviously, any wage settlement has to be related to the profits of the company, its competitive situation, the market condition at the time, other needs for plant expansion or depreciation, etc. Thus, a company decision is the result of a balancing of all these needs and claims. None are met or solved perfectly and completely. The hope is that all are partly met, and yet it is acknowledged that none are fully realized. So how can one claim perfection and an easy right or wrong? Given the economic system and its methods, one does the best one can, but it is obvious that one cannot claim that one's best is unambiguously right.

So now the question is whether there is any other alternative to all this moral agonizing within given options? And here I come to the main issue of this letter. For my reply to the query is that there is an additional alternative. I use the word "additional" rather than "other" because I believe we shall always have to make moral decisions within given contexts, practices, systems and procedures. But I am now arguing that *in addition,* the Christian ethic calls upon us to criticize the system, the "givens," and to change them when necessary and possible. Thus, I have criticized the concepts of progress and production. For many people, increased production and a proper rate of growth is a "given," an axiom, a basic part of our economic process. And yet, if we accept this uncritically we are forced to accept all the varying pressures to produce. We are forced to expand toothpaste production as well as steel or missiles. Within this "situation" our moral choices are difficult and limited. But what is more, the very process of expansion may result in other questionable moral effects. I have tried to suggest that glutting the market with cosmetics and chrome, and the attendant methods of creating demands, raise moral problems. Now, in addition, I am arguing that it is ethically necessary to raise critical moral questions about our general process. In other words, what kind of progress? Do we not need to make some general value judgments about the relative importance of various types of goods produced? This is why I have mentioned the old concept of production for need. When this value is introduced, one can begin to apply moral insights and decisions to larger issues. One is now widening the moral horizon beyond the immediate daily decisions and company issues to the whole domain of the public interest. And obviously, the very phrase "public interest" is another ethical value of central importance.

Let me illustrate if I can the importance of such a wider value as public interest. We are all familiar with the obvious ethic of "be kind to employees within the company." Suppose we achieve a high degree of this kindness in our firm. Are we entitled to "rest at ease in some moral zion?" Not at all. While we may have achieved a pretty fair tribal moral level, it is still only tribal. So then the higher moral question is: how are we treating society, the public, the consumer? Are the high wages and lush fringe benefits of our workers given at the price of a high cost on our product? Is it right to milk the consumer for the benefit of a few workers? (I would also ask this same question of some labor unions.) If we consider seriously the value of the public interest, then we may change some of our actual economic policies within the company. For example, the old economic question is still with us: Shall we produce a few units at a large profit margin, or move many units at a smaller margin? I would argue that if we introduce the ethical value of the public interest, we would then decide to produce a large volume at lower prices. But even this decision would also be influenced by how seriously we took another moral concept, namely, public need. Thus, if I were manufacturing jewelry, I would have to ask whether the public needs more cheap necklaces. Or conversely, if I were producing cars, what does the public need, more chrome, or a first-rate, quality $1,500 vehicle? Again let me emphasize, that I am not asking us to operate purely from an ideal of public service. I am charging that too many of us have operated only from the opposite side of "what's in it for me and the company." Now I am asking, that in addition to self-interest, we also inject the ethical value of public interest. It is not a question of either naked self-interest or pure altruistic service; it is a posture of what I would call valid self-interest and necessary public morality.

Similarly, in other areas of our economic life I would apply the larger ethical concerns. For example, we are all familiar with the methods and pressures of competition. Rather than simply saying "that's the way all business is run," we need to pass critical judgment on some of the methods of competition. Hence, as I wrote to a colleague of yours, there should be limits put on the amount of pressure effected in the quota system whether it be in dry goods sales or insurance policy sales, and the methods of administering the quota system could be more just and humane. Furthermore, if some people feel that any given business or company is "just a rat race in which you run with the crowd or get fired," then it is a moral duty to raise the question as to whether the conditions and procedures of the race can be changed. If they cannot, the problem of retaining moral integrity and arriving at very narrow and ambiguous moral choices is there and it is tough. For some, it may be possible to get out and work elsewhere. For a very few, internal reform may be possible. But if neither is possible, then the moral struggle is very great. Indeed, the agony of being morally sensitive and practically helpless is enormous. But even though the degrees and intensity of moral struggle vary, the point is that there are always moral problems to be faced no matter where we work or in what vocation. Therefore, it becomes even more urgent that we raise the larger moral questions in order to see if we can change and improve the methods of competition. In short, I am saying we may be able to improve the level and quality of our moral options and climate.

At the same time, however, it would be very dangerous to imagine that by changing economic and political structures, we would then arrive at easy moral solutions and thereby come nearer to sainthood. My quarrel with the extreme economic and political Left is that they assume that social structures are the determining moral factor. They tend to assume that man is basically good, but that some social forms are bad. Therefore, they call for a radical change in economic and political systems. They believe it is possible to devise good or better structures, and by proper planning, improve the process. Man, being good, will then achieve goodness. I disagree with this view for many reasons, but especially for two basic reasons: First, I do not believe man is that good. I believe evil is present in both man and social organizations, and that any system can and will be corrupted in varying degrees by men. Secondly, I do not believe it is possible for planners to plan effective blueprints in advance, nor administrate them fairly en route. The problem of the power of the planners is the problem of sin, and I have never yet read any adequate description in "socialist" literature which recognized the need for checks and balances on the planners. I might add that the problem of planning is not limited to government but is a perennial problem in management too. Anyway, we cannot go into the whole area of political and economic theory here. Suffice it to say that I do not agree with many "leftists" who see evil largely in terms of external social arrangements.

On the other hand, I have to disagree with the extreme conservative Right who, oddly enough, agree on some basic points with the Left, but come to different conclusions. Most Right-Wingers also assert the basic goodness of man and stress the individual virtues of freedom, initiative, will power, go-gettingness and achievement. As with the Left, so the Right also tends to regard social structures as evil. Therefore they call for the least possible amount of system and order. The source of evil is thus identified externally in society. Thus, the hope of man is to be left alone to work out his own destiny in terms of enlightened self-interest. From these assumptions follow the call for unrestrained free enterprise, the open market, little government and no welfare. I disagree with this view for the same reasons as before, namely, I do not believe man is that good. The doctrine of sin tells me that we are not as enlightened as we think, that self-interest can be terribly destructive, and that man needs some control on his egoism and powers. I do not believe that evil resides only in social structures, and not in man. All of life is a mixture of good and evil, and some economic and political systems are better than others. But the absence or minimum presence of social arrangements is not necessarily better, and it may be worse. In our day, for instance, it is at least a debatable question whether railroads should be run by a private corporation or by the government. The point is that it is not automatically more moral for railroads to be run by either party. It is a complex debate and I believe either answer would be something less than perfect morally and economically. Finally, I quarrel with the extreme Right because I find no concept or concern for public interest. Their philosophy is appealing only to the strong and the successful. For their system is a huge struggle between competitive individuals in which only the mighty reach the top. The rest are consigned to their lot, with sermons against laziness, coddling, inefficiency, and inferiority. There is, in short, no social responsibility, no love. And I think it significant to note that most Right-Wingers in our culture are quite well-off and quite successful. It is easy to say "leave me alone" when you're on top.

So, as you can see, here I am in another middle ground position. For I believe in the need for individual freedom, struggle and initiative. I have no desire to reduce anyone to a common denominator, to put him in a mediocre mold economically, politically, or religiously. At the same time, I believe that social structures can achieve greater levels of social justice and order. By social structures I mean both government action, policies and laws, and various group organizations such as PTA's, professional societies and charitable outfits, etc. I do not trust any individual with too much power, nor do I trust any government or organization with too much power. I, as an individual, can and should do a lot about my own duties and responsibilities. But some social units and group action can perform other duties and responsibilities a lot better. A purely social salvation and ethic overlook individual freedoms and duties. A purely individual ethic overlooks social, public and national duties and responsibilities.

If you agree with these general but very basic theological observations and join me in the middle ground position, then we can get back to other equally basic and difficult ethical problems. For please note, in all the questions I raised in the previous paragraph, there are vast areas of important debatable issues. For instance, what parts of our political structure are more good than bad, and vice versa? More specifically in economics, which taxes are relatively good, which relatively unjust? Or what aspects of life are my responsibility, and what aspects can be better handled by groups, social or governmental? Or note that I have often used the phrase, "business and government partnership." Well, how should they cooperate? Which economic decisions should be made by management, which by government, and which jointly? And watch out for the word "partnership," for all is not always lovey-dovey, even in families. Therefore, we need checks and balances, freedom and order. But how and where and who is able to define clearly and by what authority?

Well, I trust you see the issue here. Having rejected the doctrinaire and childishly simple slogans of the Right and Left, I do not end up with another simple uncomplicated answer. All the problems are still with us, the everyday practical moral problems as well as the larger ethical issues. But I believe we shall be better equipped to decide and to act more morally when we avoid false either/ors, and understand what are the real issues confronting us, the general as well as the specific problems.

Middle-manly yours, etc.

— 19 —

Mr. Eric Cosdale
The Fern Glen Realty Company
Suburbia, U.S.A.

Dear Mr. Cosdale:

Your letter of last Wednesday was refreshing in its candor and in its specific practical problem presented. You say you agree with me, in general, that Christianity calls for both individual freedom and social responsibility. Or to put it another way, we seem to agree that purely private morals, however adequate and noble, do not go very far toward solving social issues. On the other hand, we also concur that purely external social arrangements, systems, laws and plans, however noble and well-planned, do not solve the stubborn issues of corruption, individual sin and motive. Finally, we both seem to arrive at that respectable but vague middle ground position where we assert that we need both individual and social ethics. And we acknowledge that a balance is needed, that sometimes the delicate balance teeters too much one way or the other, and that it is the duty of the Christian to right the balance.

Well, all this is very well, you say, but like most general statements, it is not very helpful when you are faced with a concrete problem. And the one you raise is, indeed, a difficult one! You are a real estate man in an average suburban community. Like most such parts of town, it is composed chiefly of average middle or upper middle class families and it is an all-white group. Problem: a Negro family wants in; what do you do?

I was delighted to see that you did not adopt the usual solutions which are so widely practiced. One answer, of course, is to quietly but firmly refuse to sell any house or apartment to a Negro. This can be done very effectively and without any unfavorable publicity. A realtor can simply refuse, tell the colored applicant in plain language, and give no reasons for the refusal. Or one can refuse in more polite terms by placing the blame on "a city ordinance," or "a long-time town custom." The inference here is that the individual realtor is sympathetic to the Negro but the law or the custom of the town is what prevents any possible sale. By this ruse, the realtor hopes to deceive the Negro and/or himself into believing that he, the individual realtor, is a good moral person, even if the town isn't. Or still another answer is the old familiar "Gentlemen's Agreement." Here all the real estate agencies get together and all agree not to sell to any Negroes or any other agreed upon undesirables. Naturally, there is no written policy; it's just a verbal gentlemen's understanding. It is often further strengthened by enlisting the support of the local banks, especially the mortgage officers. This neighborhood pact is also very efficient and lets each individual participant off the moral hook. The banker can say that he is not averse to letting Negroes in but "the real estate men are against it, you know." And, of course, the realtors can return the compliment. However, if neither the realtors nor the bankers see fit to put the blame on each other and prefer to hold on to a common front together, there is another "fall guy"—public opinion. Surely, you have heard this phrase many times, Mr. Cosdale: "You know me, Eric. I have nothing against the good Negroes—like that Dr. Johnson—he's a fine man. But if I sold him a house in Fernwood, everybody would raise hell. I tell you, the public wouldn't stand for it."

There are doubtless many other variations on these refusals. As Christians, how shall we respond to these practices and their rationalizations? From what you say in your letter, I am sure we agree that we reject the first position. To refuse any person a chance to buy or rent a house purely on the grounds of race is clearly un-Christian. There is nothing in the Bible or in the heart of the Christian faith which asserts the superiority of one race over another. There is nothing which says that one can judge any person for good or ill solely by his racial make-up. God has no favorite races; geography does not determine where a person must live. These are strong and, I hope, clear statements. But I believe this is one issue upon which one can take a clear and definite stand. There is no middle ground here. The Christian faith is definite here. Racism is out.

Having said all this, one could go on and write several books on our present Negro situation, segregation versus integration, sit-ins, Freedom Riders, etc. Obviously I cannot deal with these momentous issues here. But in a small way I believe the real estate problem is a microscopic illustration of the basic issues in the larger problems in the South. And just in case we Northern Yankees think of race only in terms of the South, let us now also substitute, in our little example, the Jewish race. And again, we Christians will have to say the same thing: We have no right to deny any person the right to buy or rent a house simply because of race or color. This is *the* Christian position. There is no qualifying it or watering it down. To the extent that we compromise on it, change it, make exceptions, to that extent we deny our faith. Therefore, it is good to know that you stand foursquare on this basic Christian ethical principle.

You say that as a Christian, you too believe that there should be no real estate restriction directed against any person solely because of race or color. But you also describe the fact that you seem to be virtually alone in this conviction. You go on to point out that if you did sell a house to a Negro or Jew, you would probably be ostracized socially, and what is worse, you would doubtless lose your business. Therefore, you ask me the concrete question of what should or can you do?

We have already agreed that you cannot remain silent and go along with your present neighborhood practice of discrimination. On the other hand, you are frank to admit that you are not ready to suffer the martyrdom of business failure and social isolation. Thus, you ask whether any middle ground choice means a compromise or lessening of your Christian faith.

I believe an answer has already been shown by some ethical pioneers. The procedure is something like this: You find one or two or five or six other people who share your conviction. Who are these persons? One may be a minister, another a doctor, a lawyer, a businessman, or a labor foreman. They may be Christian, or Jewish, or agnostic, or atheistic. At this point, it does not matter what their formal faith or what their vocation or politics. If you can find a small group of people who agree on this issue, this is where you begin.

Next, you meet together, decide what to do, and assign responsible jobs. For instance, each person is usually a member of some organization, or at least has some friends who may share this particular conviction. This small group can thus expand its interest by word of mouth. But further, a statement can be drawn up, even a fairly general one. It can be printed on cards and distributed to members of churches, Rotary Clubs, business groups. These people are asked to consider the statement, and if they can agree with it, to sign the card and to stand by their signature. I think you will be surprised how many will sign such a pledge, a pledge to support an Open Housing Covenant.

Now thus far perhaps this sounds like an elaborate way to get people to support a noble but futile resolution. If we stopped with that, you would be right. But we do not. The real point of enlisting even a minority of people in town is to show that "public opinion" is *not* all in favor of discrimination. Members of the original committee can then go to the real estate operators and bankers and show that part of the public is in favor of an open housing covenant. Let's be frank. This *is* a kind of pressure. But unlike social prejudice, this is an open, honest, and clear pressure exerted by responsible people. There are no tricks, no threats, no economic boycotts.

Other things can be done. There is a great deal of information available to show what has, in fact, happened to other communities which have opened their real estate doors. For example, a common argument against an open door policy is that "the neighborhood will deteriorate and taxes to the town decline." Factual studies show that such is not the case. The vast majority of cases prove that the neighborhood either remains the same or improves in quality. There are one or two instances where the area did decline for a while, but then regained its status.

You can make clear that you know there are undesirable neighbors, but that such families are *not* undesirable because they are of another race or color. It is an obvious fact that some Christians, some Protestants, are undesirable in the sense that we do not like them, or do not agree with their tastes or habits. The point is that it is individual people who are desirable or undesirable, *not* races or classes. And the way to deal with undesirables is on a personal basis, not by restrictive codes which apply only to whole groups of people. And by the way, who determines who is "desirable" or not, and by what standard?

So what I am trying to emphasize is that it is possible to solve restrictive housing policies. I do not say that it is easy or that you or anyone else can automatically solve it in your neighborhood. Some places may be so dogmatically and fanatically prejudiced that nothing can be done now. On the other hand, I believe that in many cases, the situation is not that bad. In most instances, the chief enemies are fear and lethargy. When a small groups gets on the ball, they will find that a fairly large mass of people will respond and move just enough to make it all possible and effective.

As you can see, this housing issue is a good example or illustration of the old conflict between the Christian ethic and the culture of a society. It is not enough to try to be "a good Christian" all alone. If the particular culture in our particular neighborhood is virtually one hundred percent in favor of closed and discriminatory housing, the "one good Christian" faces martyrdom if he acts. If he remains silent and goes along with the crowd, he violates his own integrity and furthers the prejudice. Therefore, it seems to me that some kind of minority group action, as suggested above, is a way to challenge and criticize the culture. This is why the prophetic tradition within Christianity is so essential. For a part of the job of the Christian faith is to judge culture. We believe that it is our duty to try and transform such a culture. And our point is that we cannot do it alone—as individuals.

So in your situation, it may well be that a move on your part does involve some risk. Your business might suffer a temporary drop; it might not, but it is a real possibility. On the other hand, your business may increase, and this has happened. But I cannot say, from this easy chair, "go to it, all will be well, you will succeed and be an even finer Christian." The particular way suggested in this letter has worked in the vast majority of communities in which it was tried. The chances of it succeeding in your neighborhood can only be adequately estimated by you who live there. As a general rule, the plan goes far better than expected. On the other hand, this Open Housing Covenant method is not a cure-all, and it may not work everywhere. Other ways may be found which are more effective and suitable for some neighborhoods. But I am sure you see the point, namely, that silence is not enough. One can at least begin exploratory conversations with some other people. Raise the issue, state your convictions and concern, and some seeds may be planted which will bear fruit.

Yours for a good planting, etc.

— 20 —

MR. THOMAS BOND
AMERICAN PUBLISHING CO.
MILWAUKEE, WISCONSIN

Dear Mr. Bond:

Your letter arrived this morning and your comments I found to be most discerning and fair. You waste no time in pointing out with refreshing frankness the weaknesses in my position. You note especially the debatable conclusions I offer on many specific moral issues. But the most basic question you raise seems to me to be the problem of diversity among Christians. You say that you are a Christian, that you believe the same (roughly) theological and ethical principles that I do, and that you sincerely try to apply them and put them into practice. Yet you come up with different answers. If I read you correctly, you do not like this, and wish that all Christians could agree and thereby make clear our virtues and unite on particular actions.

Let me first say that I share your concern, and wish that we could have more concerted action and more clear-cut moral virtues. While I believe we can improve our performance on these matters, I also believe there are important reasons why diversity and debate are not all bad or undesirable. Nevertheless, it is important to analyze why there is disagreement between sincere Christians on most moral decisions. One reason lies in the area of just plain technical knowledge. If the moral problem before us concerns a more equitable tax law or wage policy, certain basic facts are involved. If I do not know much about the tax situation and its laws, I could hardly come up with an intelligent or relevant decision. In such instances, the relatively ignorant person proposes some vague moral resolution to the effect that taxes should be more just or that there should be less taxes all around. The most such a statement could produce is some pressure for a general tax review or investigation. But it offers little help or guidance on any practical or specific level. For clearly it does not deal with the real issues such as which taxes are unjust, how one can reduce taxes and support needed expenditures, and how one decides, specifically, where improvement is needed. I am saying, then, that one cannot even make a relevant decision unless he knows the facts of the situation. Therefore, the less informed Christian will likely come to a different and more vague general conclusion than the well informed Christian.

Yet it is obvious that we cannot be expertly or even adequately informed on all possible issues. You know more about business and economics than I do; I may know more about foreign policy and politics than you do. And both of us have to make moral decisions in all these areas (when we vote, for example). Because we differ in how much we know, we may very well differ in our decisions. This does not make one person less Christian or less moral than the other. It may make us less relevant and practical. But it does underline the necessity of mutual dialogue, communication, and sharing of information and insight. Both of us are caught in the paradox of knowing that technical knowledge is necessary to inform our moral choices, and yet also knowing that we never can get all the knowledge we would like to have. It is irresponsible to say that we will only make a decision when all the evidence is in, or when a wholly right solution appears. Obviously, all the evidence is never in and *the* perfect solution never appears. Thus we must continue to make moral decisions, incomplete and imperfect though they may be. This is the human condition and it is one reason for our differences.

Another reason for diversity is the individual's background. All of us are brought up differently in different home situations, cultural values and biases. I would insist that the Christian faith can rescue us from our provincial and personal biases, outlook and attitudes. For when the God in Christ is taken seriously, all our values and attitudes are judged by Him and His yardstick. But I would never argue that we can be completely rescued from our upbringing. The "old man" of the past is always with us in varying degrees. Thus, if I am brought up in a relatively comfortable suburban environment, I will not have the same outlook as someone brought up in a steel-worker's family in Gary, Indiana. This is not to say that one outlook is necessarily better or worse than the other; it is only to point to the obvious differences. But this is another way of saying that nobody, including the Christian, can be absolutely objective about anything. The personal equation and history are always there, and they account for part of our differences.

A third cause for diversity in moral decisions is that, as you probably know, there is seldom any one right and complete answer to a problem. There may be several relatively good answers. For example, how should an employer express love and justice towards his employees? Surely one could not say that there is only one right way to express love and concern. There are many possibilities: higher wages, more fringe benefits, more personal contacts, more consultation and communication, etc. Furthermore, in deciding which actions to take, a knowledge of the situation is important.

If, for instance, the employer had just given the employees a large wage raise, it is unlikely that we would then say that *the* answer is another raise. And even if that were so, one could hardly say that there were no other possibilities of expressing concern. Similarly, let us say that you and I believe in equal justice for all men regardless of race, color, or creed. It is obvious that there are many cases of injustice. The problem is how to correct the injustices. One of us might say that only a federal law with power can effect the proper change. Another might say that only in a gradual way can local authorities adequately deal with the issue. Neither of us can prove in advance which policy would be better. Moreover, in one case, federal law might be more effective; in another case, it might be worse. Neither of us can foresee the future, nor know the complexities of each case. Therefore, there are the mutual limitations of our finitude, ignorance, biases and the varieties of the external situations. So obviously there is diversity. And equally obviously, neither of us can claim that our advocated policy is the right one, or even the best. We may wish it were otherwise, but it cannot be.

Thus far we have offered a few reasons why sincere Christians differ on specific moral decisions. We have assumed that the Christians begin with roughly the same theological and ethical principles. But what if Christians differ honestly in their basic theological convictions? My reply would then be that this would constitute another cause of diversity. If I have a quite optimistic view of human nature and a large trust in reason, my moral decisions will differ from a Christian who is fairly pessimistic about human nature and who has little trust in objective reason. But here again, each person would run into situations in which his particular view would have to be modified. For clearly, one could not trust everyone under all circumstances, nor could one overlook the possibility of at least partly rational improvements. In short, there are times when one should be very realistic and tough-minded, and other times when some vision and hope are equally essential.

Now what is the upshot of all this analysis of diversity among Christians, let alone people of other persuasions? I would suggest that the following conclusions are essential: Since it should be obvious by now that all of us are both finite and sinful, humility becomes us. This means on the highest level that someone cannot say that his basic theological beliefs are wholly right and completely true, that my theological descriptions are all right and yours all wrong. No one can say that his words exhaust the nature of God. Similarly, all descriptions of love or beauty are less than the reality we are attempting to describe. It is necessary, therefore, that we compare notes, that we remain open to the descriptions and experiences of others. On the secondary level of ethical principles, we can apparently reach agreement. For all of us will avow justice, freedom, love, integrity, etc. Yet as soon as someone starts defining or describing these principles he runs into the same problem, namely, are our descriptions adequate and the only true ones? Clearly, we could not make such a claim, and therefore, we need the wisdom of others. And on the third level of moral decisions and applications of ethical principles, we have already shown diversity. Thus, it is essential that we do not make claims of infallibility or righteousness, or sole authority. We are all less than perfect, and in order to avoid arrogant claims of superiority, humility is what keeps us where we belong. But more important, it keeps us open to new insights and wisdom and sharing from fellow Christians and others.

A second conclusion to be drawn from this diversity is to note that it is not necessarily undesirable or uncreative. While it would appear that a vast unified agreement would move mountains and hold up to the public a great clear witness, such unity in action assumes that there is a clearly right answer to a problem. We have seen that there are few problems with only one simply right answer. To claim that there is such an answer is, in fact, to cut off any other answer. For example, if I say that *the* Christian answer to the national financial problems is to balance the budget, then by definition, all other answers are un-Christian and wrong. This black and white approach actually prevents other possible creative solutions. Thus, a too insistent call for unity often results in destructive action because it rules out many complex but more adequate and realistic solutions.

By contrast, a diversified approach tends to evoke many suggested answers, a pooling of wisdom and insight, an attitude of flexibility, and a readiness to change. Democratic discussion and group decisions are based on the assumption that each individual has a part of the truth, and that the pooled wisdom is better than the judgment of an isolated individual. Of course, there is danger in diversity and group action. Sometimes a group decision is a lowest common denominator agreement. And one individual may have a superior insight. Further, the rights and freedom of the individual must be protected. It is also true that there is the danger of divisiveness. The trick lies in the proper attitude of people. If individuals use diversity as a contest for waging their private ego wars, the results are destructive. But if humility and concern are dominant, diversity can be creative. Therefore, it seems to me that we have to walk a difficult tightrope between common principles and relative and varied moral actions. We shall always be tempted to abandon the tightrope in one of two ways. Either we are beguiled into the laziness of feeling that, because problems are so difficult, and because there is so much diversity, nothing can be done. This is the escape into sceptical relativism. It is the lazy attitude which says: "What's the use, nobody knows the answers, everybody differs and nothing can be done." Or, because we do not like the insecurity and difficulty of complexity, we are tempted to believe that there are definite and simple answers. Thus, many people buy dogmatic and authoritarian systems, religious or secular, left or right. When this occurs, tyranny and fanaticism reign, and then we are really in trouble.

My plea, then, in this letter is to say that the Christian faith enables us to live with diversity in a creative way. The Christian way is a diversity within a unity. The unity is our common humility and creatureliness before God, our common devotion to the call for love and justice. The diversity is the way each of us seeks to apply love and justice to our everyday actions. It's something like the relations between the sexes: only a fanatic would say that there is only one way to love; only a cynic would say that there is no way; but the lover would prove that there are many ways.

Yours for loving actions, etc.

— 21 —

MR. WILLIAM REYNOLDS
APEX MERCHANDISING CORP.
MARLINVILLE, OHIO

Dear Mr. Reynolds:

Your letter arrived by Special Delivery this morning. I must say I was surprised by the urgency of delivery! And you make it quite clear that you were surprised at compromise. Imagine a Christian minister declaring the need for compromise in morality! Well, aside from exclamation points and Special Delivery, you do raise a very basic and much misunderstood problem and I shall try to clarify what I believe to be the Christian view on compromise.

First of all, the popular use of the word "compromise" usually connotes the abandonment of morality. For example, when someone says, "I will not compromise on that issue," he usually means that he will not give up his position. Similarly, when someone remarks that "John Doe compromised himself in that situation," he usually means that Mr. Doe abandoned his moral integrity, gave in, and went along with the crowd or succumbed to some pressure. Now, when the word compromise is used in such examples, I would join you in rejecting it. I, too, would be against any abandonment of moral standards. The Christian ethic is against giving up a call for justice and replacing it by a me-first in the name of my freedom. Thus, if compromise means give up, then I am against it.

However, I have tried to make clear that there is another meaning to the word compromise. I have described many situations in which there is no perfect moral choice. A political election is the most obvious example. Voting for either party involves an ambiguous decision because neither party is perfectly good. And a refusal to vote because of evils in both parties, lands one in the evil of irresponsibility. So whatever one does on election day is mixed with good and evil, as our own internal motives are. Therefore, I say that a vote is a compromise, that is, it is a choice of the lesser of two evils, or, if you prefer, a vote for the relatively better party. The word "compromise" here means the recognition that my moral choice is less than perfect. It does *not* mean that I am giving up all moral considerations. Or to put it another way, compromise means seeking the most moral solution but with the awareness that all solutions are less than perfect.

Because of the confusion over the word compromise, I am perfectly willing to abandon the word altogether. But I believe it is essential to retain the problem and the Christian answer to the problem. Negatively speaking, it is necessary for the Christian to know, in advance, that he cannot make an absolutely right moral choice in anything. Why? Because almost all moral choices in life are mixtures of good and evil, shades of gray. And internally, our motives and attitudes are mixtures of good and evil. No external situation is perfect; no internal personality is without sin. Therefore, let us not deceive ourselves into imagining that we are morally pure and our moral decision is absolutely right. "If we say we have no sin, we deceive ourselves, and the truth is not in us" (I John 1:8). This negative way of stating part of the problem is essential in order to safeguard us from fanatical claims of self-righteousness and the idolatrous simple answer method of the good guys versus the bad guys.

Positively speaking, the Christian seeks the best possible moral solution. He is not content with the easiest answer. The Christian gospel demands that we go beyond, or try to go beyond, the law of society. Indeed it is encouraging to note that some people are beginning to raise the question in this form, "Though it may be legally correct, is it ethically right?" This question was raised in the late 1950's over the issue of the conflict of interests for businessmen entering government service. But the question is a valid one for all of us wherever we are. There may be no legal or social law to cover a number of moral dilemmas. Because there is no civil law does not mean I am free to do whatever I can get away with. As a Christian, there is a higher law which demands my obedience. Therefore, I seek to do what is possible in terms of Christ's call for love and justice. Negative Christian realism, such as the doctrine of sin, informs me of the complexities of the problem at hand, but positive Christian love and justice impel me to seek the best possible, the most nearly right answer. Rather than use the word compromise to describe this situation, some have said that this approach is Christian realism. For want of a better phrase, let's use that one. But regardless of labels or phrases, I hope the basic problem is at least partly clarified. Perhaps we could summarize it this way: The Christian is called upon to take Christ's perfect love and apply it to imperfect situations with imperfect motives. The recognition of this situation is not the abandonment of morality. Quite the contrary, it is effective morality in action.

A fuller understanding of this type of Christian morality leads us to deeper considerations of the nature of Christian ethics. Anyone who wants to take the Christian ethic seriously must begin with Christian theology. For it is theology which gives us the basic descriptions and interpretations of the basic issues in life. It is theology which tells us about the nature of man, what God is like, how He is known through Christ, what the will of God is for man, and what our relation is with God and our fellow men. Theology describes the problem of power, the power of sin in us, the need for forgiveness, the ways of love and justice. Surely these problems are *the* basic ones. If a man does not subscribe to these Christian affirmations, he will subscribe to some other interpretations of the nature of life. And it is these basic issues which will determine the kind of ethic and morality he will follow. Let me illustrate this point by an extreme example: if a man believes that there is no God and that all men are really nothing but complicated animals determined by natural forces and dominated by self-interest, then his ethics and morality will be egoistic and self-centered. He will be out for all he can get and get away with. Since he believes everyone else is doing the same thing, why should he help others or feel any restraint upon his own methods and goals? Thus, it seems clear to me that a man's theology, his basic views about basic issues in life, determines what kind of ethics and morality he adopts and uses. So, in Christianity we begin with our theology. From these basic affirmations, we then derive our ethics.

The Christian ethic is the demand for love and justice. It is the care, concern and action for ourselves, our neighbors and our God. But now the problem is: how does one apply and live out love and justice? This immediately forces us into concrete moral choices and actions. I believe that moral virtues help us to apply love and justice to everyday particular situations. Honesty, integrity, prudence, wisdom, truth-telling, and sincerity are guides to moral action. Taken by themselves, however, these virtues are not adequate. For they are similar to noble ideals. They may tell us what is ideal and relatively good, but they do not give us the power to realize them. Furthermore, no one of them can handle a complex situation, nor can all of them together solve the problem of conflicting demands. Whether, for example, to tell the truth to a patient dying of cancer, cannot be decided purely on the grounds of honesty. Other considerations enter in, such as, whether the patient can take the bad news, will it make him better or worse, etc. And this type of consideration I would put under the domain of love. Love and concern for the patient will determine how much truth should be told and in what way. Thus, the moral virtues of honesty and truth-telling come under the criterion of love. Love is the theological-ethical absolute or yardstick; the moral virtues are relative to love. To say, "Always tell the truth no matter what," is to absolutize truth, and sometimes, therefore, even to deny love by being cruel. Yet, moral virtues do have their proper place and are useful, though relative guides.

I also believe the moral virtues serve the function of judging and reminding us that we cannot always be perfectly honest, brave, loyal, sincere, and truthful. If we take virtues and ideals seriously, they should keep us humble, and by themselves they show us what ought to be but do not give us the power to do the good. We cannot simply say that love and justice are all we need. I believe it is also essential to try to achieve the moral virtues. If love is our only guide, then it is very easy to say that I did the most loving possible thing in a given situation and let it go at that. If the moral dilemma is very complex, I believe we need to know where we had to "compromise." Without the judgment of the moral virtues, we shall be tempted to believe that since love was present it wasn't much of a compromise after all. Then we slide into pride.

The really difficult job for the Christian is to keep a proper balance between his theology, his ethic, moral virtues and concrete action. Here are some of the ways in which the balance can be upset. One extreme is to concentrate on theology exclusively, on various views about the nature of God, man, salvation, worship—in short, reading and thinking about formal theological concepts. Others who do not find theological writings to their taste may be concerned with ecclesiastical or liturgical matters. Thus, some church laymen have pretty strict notions about who is orthodox or not, what is the right way to conduct a service or run a parish. The emphasis is always on outward forms of the faith. An exclusive interest here usually neglects "the weightier matters of the Law."

Another version of the same extreme is called pietism. Here the attention is focused chiefly on one's personal relation to God as expressed in private prayer, meditation and worship. A common expression of this approach is to assert that since religion is purely personal and private, the Church should avoid controversy and stick to purely spiritual things. This view is an imbalance because it totally ignores the prophetic tradition of Christianity, our ethical responsibility to love our neighbor and to reform society in order to extend justice. This view, in other words, is open to the charge of "Sunday Christian; week-day pagan."

At the opposite pole of these two forms of withdrawal from the affairs of the world is the moralistic view which asserts that all one needs is a clear code of right and wrong, that it isn't what a man believes, but what he does that counts. This view assumes that it is relatively easy to formulate simple rules of conduct and to apply them to everyday problems. Let me repeat that the Christian faith insists that there are no simple moral choices. The idea that there are simple moral answers of easy right and wrong to most of life's problems is incredibly naive. I am sure you do not subscribe to this Boy Scout view of morality.

Another version of this extreme is the philosophy of good intentions and the avoidance of obvious evils. Thus, a man is tempted to say, "I meant well" or, "I did my best, so who can ask for anything more?" Of course intentions are important and all of us want to do our best. But if we use these as an excuse for wrongs committed or our inaction, then it won't do. Such clichés are preludes to pride, and William James' classic rejoinder comes to mind: "The road to hell is paved with good intentions." That may be an extreme statement, but there is truth in it. The truth is that we cannot rest on these moral oars. Nor can we say that because we didn't do an obvious evil, therefore we are obviously good.

These, then, are some examples of an extreme imbalance in theology, ethics and morality. As to what is *the* right balance, one cannot easily describe it. And the proper mixture of the three parts will vary and should vary with individuals and particular situations. Some individuals are gifted with high intellectual ability. For them, the balance should probably be in the direction of theology. They are best equipped to deal with such tough problems as the relation between science and faith, or marxist challenges to Christian theology and so on. Other individuals are gifted for more practical concerns and direct action. They should be involved in building, organizing, directing, doing things. But both need the advice and corrections of the other. The theologian needs to be confronted with the practical problems of everyday living. The activist needs to consider the deeper issues behind particular actions: their purpose, the effects, the morality, the why of it all.

Or, the balance may be altered in any given social situation. There are times when careful analysis of a problem is essential. There are other times when vigorous action is needed. And obviously one cannot always do the same thing; constant action without evaluation may lead to trouble. Similarly, continual analysis may lead to no action at all, or as someone has said "paralysis by analysis." So my conclusion here is that the full Christian way means that we keep a flexible balance of *theology*—basic answers to basic problems, worship, prayer, faith; *ethics*—the basic principles and power of love and justice; *morality*—the guiding virtues; and *action*—putting all these things into practice. This is why Christianity is not just a theology, or a code, or a set of ideals, or a system or an organization, but a way of life.

Wayfully yours, etc.

— 22 —

MR. JOHN B. ENTERPRISE
THE NATIONAL BUSINESSMEN'S ASSOCIATION
ANYWHERE, U.S.A.

Dear Mr. Enterprise:

I shall be glad to respond to your request for a summary of the letters I have written to some of your acquaintances. Acknowledging in advance the inevitable weaknesses of all such summaries, the danger of over-simplification and one-sided statements, I shall give it a try.

There are, it seems to me, several widespread attitudes about the relation of Christianity to business which are very dangerous and very antithetical to Christianity and to business itself. One view seems to hold that there can be no fruitful mixture of Christianity and business. Business is a vigorous, competitive process; it runs by its own natural economic laws of the market, and no one could survive by forgiveness and turning the other cheek. The upholders of this position are not necessarily anti-religious. Many businessmen attend church and are sincere in their personal faith and devotion. But they see no connection between Christianity and their business or economics and politics. Some few wish there were such a connection; others are insistent that there should be no relation. And most people in this group do not want the Church to meddle in economic and social problems. As someone has said, "The ideal church for some American businessmen is the Russian Orthodox Church; it avoids all controversy and sticks only to 'spiritual' matters of almost total irrelevance."

I believe that this divorce of Christianity from business and social life is a tragic mistake. For one thing, I would argue that such a separation is a gross misunderstanding of the Christian faith. It is a denial of the whole prophetic tradition in the Bible, it is a denial of the very nature of love as taught and exemplified by Christ, and it reduces religion to a private little corner of life, thereby rendering Christianity useless and irrelevant. What is worse, this view tends to make Christianity into a kind of sop and balm to the conscience, or provide a pleasant aesthetic and spiritual escape from reality and everyday life. Surely Christ did not die for that. Christianity has always asserted that Christ is the Lord of all of life, not just a tiny part of it. Surely the Almighty God does not exist only to give us pleasant feelings once in a while. If we say religion has no relevance to economic or political life, we are saying that God is either absent or a tiny god, while the real power in life is nature or economics or man. Such a god is not worth worshipping. In short, a separation between Christianity and the major parts of life is a denial of the Christian faith.

An opposite and equally widespread view on the relation of Christianity to business is to hold that there is no real problem involved. This group believes Christianity is and can be related to business very easily. A prominent business leader has been quoted as saying that he runs his company strictly according to the Sermon on the Mount and the Golden Rule. Other men have testified that the Ten Commandments and the Rule really do work; in fact, it is good business to employ the principles of the Sermon on the Mount. Still others tend to equate Christianity with free enterprise, democracy, capitalism, and the American Way of Life. When one compares our system to other economic processes such as marxism, isn't it obvious that ours is more moral? It is also easy to point to obvious evils and evildoers, and by comparison conclude that we are obviously good and religious. Thus, this group argues that Christianity and our business system are virtually the same. And if one criticizes this position, the defenders frequently label the critics un-American and anti-Christian. When this occurs the identification is complete.

My quarrel with this position is that it too fails to understand the full nature of Christianity. This view also denies or ignores the whole prophetic tradition of the Bible. It will not tolerate or seriously consider the prophetic critic. But what is worse, this view is guilty of a terrible pride because it equates our system with God. It also provides an easy conscience for the individual businessman. In his self-deception, he seems to believe that he is living up to the Golden Rule and the Sermon on the Mount. But any awareness of the nature of sin should inform us that no one is that good. And because I do not commit an obvious evil such as murder does not mean that I am obviously good in all other areas of my life. Further, our own ambiguities and evils cannot be overlooked just because Russia or China has worse evils. I am not arguing that America is as bad as those countries. I am only pointing out that we are not entitled to ignore our weaknesses just because somebody else is more evil. Jesus made this point quite clear in his criticism of the Pharisees. They were not the dregs of society by any means. On the contrary, they were among the morally best and most religious people of their time. Their chief sin was pride in their virtue and religiosity, and it is this moral and spiritual pride which Christ attacked. It is the most dangerous form of sin precisely because it precludes any future growth and depth, and because it cuts one off from other people. It is a denial of love. Let me put it bluntly and simply: if someone believes he is doing all right, he will not want to change, nor will he accept any serious criticism. Further, he will regard critics, and those of any differing views, as inferior and as a threat to him. Fear, suspicion and hatred will develop. His own position will become rigid and solidified. And the final form of blasphemy occurs when a man claims God is on his side. By definition, the opponent thus becomes the devil.

It should be obvious, therefore, that any equating of Christianity with *anything:* myself, my virtue, business, democracy, the Church, etc., is idolatry and a denial of God. No matter how good these aspects of life may be, they are not good enough. "None is good (enough) save the Father." Surely this is a central part of the Gospel of Christ.

There are, then, these two opposite extreme views on the problem of Christianity and business. If you can join me in rejecting both positions, then our job is to see how the faith can be related. My letters to you have made suggestions and given examples of how I believe Christianity and business are related. I have used two approaches. One approach has been to assume that most of us do our daily jobs within certain given situations, such as, the general procedures of our company, the market, traditional policies and so on. Within this framework, I have tried to raise the moral questions and dilemmas, and suggest some answers. My emphasis has been on how tremendously difficult and relative our decisions are, how limited and imperfect our alternatives, and how essential, therefore, it is that we understand the need for forgiveness, for humility and strength to endure such ambiguities and pressures.

I hope you felt throughout that I was sympathetic and understanding toward the enormous moral complexities facing any businessman who takes the Christian ethic seriously. I acknowledged that there is always room for legitimate difference of opinion among

Christians, and that there is no one perfect solution. I tried to stress the need for all of us to be open and tolerant and humble toward each other, and for more sharing and communication in arriving at our business and moral decisions. I believe this is the sensitive loving aspect of the Christian faith. This is a Gospel of Love which seeks to understand, to forgive, to encourage, to improve, and to redeem us. But there is another part of the Gospel too.

The other half of the Christian faith is the tough side. And because it is difficult and sometimes unpleasant, we are most likely to ignore and overlook it. The old Biblical phrases about sin, the judgment of God, wrath, etc., are regarded as relics of the past. Our contemporary popular versions of Christianity stress love and happiness, consolation and peace of mind. The few authentic prophetic voices in Christianity are ignored or dismissed with the label "doom and gloom men." The fact is, however, that Christianity is neither a religion of doom, nor is it a religion of comfort. I have tried to describe the loving and forgiving side, but I would not be true to the faith unless the other side was also presented. This is the prophetic part of Christianity. It is clearly described in the prophets of the Old Testament. In the New Testament, the tradition is furthered and exemplified in Christ. Jesus declares the absolute demands of love and justice, the primacy of God's sovereign rule, the necessity of seeking righteousness. Translated to our situation, this means that we are required by our Lord to measure our total life and culture with the yardstick of love and justice. In my earliest letters I did not raise the question of our common methods, practices and customs in business. I said they were "the given situation," rules of the game. Within these rules I tried to show the moral dilemmas we face and suggested some answers. Now, however, I am saying that Christianity calls for judgment on methods, customs and situations, on the very rules of the game. Thus, in some of my later letters, I raised the ethical questions about production for need as well as profit, about methods of advertising and sales procedures and pressures, and about the public interest. These were broad and general issues dealing with our basic culture and values. The Christian faith demands that our cultural values be critically judged. It is so very easy for any nation, any culture, any way of life to become proud and idolatrous. When this occurs, God is replaced with a tribal god, a lesser god. Of course, judgment does not mean that our values are all wrong, our culture all negative. Judgment means the discernment of what is good and bad about our way of life. It means that we should seek to preserve and improve what is good, and eliminate what is evil. The difficult job is to decide and agree on what is relatively good and relatively bad. Clearly this requires open exchange and sharing of critical judgment and evaluations. My letters were small attempts to start this process of cultural judgment from a Christian viewpoint.

If we take this prophetic side of Christianity seriously, we shall forever be uneasy and properly humble. This is the hard side of the Gospel. And we shall always be tempted to look for the soft way out, the easy conscience. If you want a pleasant, comfortable religion, do not buy the Christian faith. There are two easy religions in modern life. One is enlightened self-interest: doing what you want with supposed civility. The second is patriotism: our way of life is the best, let no one criticize or challenge us, we're doing all right. From a Christian view, these two religions are as old as man and the source of most evil. The first, basically me against you, is a war of egos. The second, essentially us against them, is a war of nation tribes. In both cases, God is left out, love and justice absent, conflict and destruction inevitable.

The Christian faith calls for all things to be judged by the God we know in Christ. By definition, all we do is less than perfect, less than right and good and true. We do not love as we ought to love, we do not extend justice far enough. We who are well off do not share enough; we do not even really know how difficult life is for the vast majority of people. Our cultural values and business practices are not good enough, some of them are really destructive. Our ulcers, frantic pace and competitive pressures testify to the fact that our lives are not as creative as they ought to be, and our anxieties about success and status reveal the loyalty and attachment to false gods.

But the Christian faith does not stop with judgment. For it is our faith that God also seeks our redemption. Therefore, judgment is the prelude to health. We must know what our illnesses are before we can be healed. The thesis of my letters is that our business life, culture and practices need the searching judgment of the Christian faith. It is insufficient to say that individual good men will improve our system. Men are not that good and the structures of the system inevitably force us into terribly ambiguous moral decisions. Nor will it do to call for the destruction of the whole business system and dream up some kind of Utopian structure. We are not wise enough to blueprint such a system, and even if we were, we are not good enough to avoid corrupting it. Therefore, we must begin to do the two difficult jobs together, simultaneously, of reforming the system and improving ourselves.

Clearly, these brief letters have not solved the problems. My hope is that they will begin a process in which we Christians, clergy and laymen together, may help each other to relate our faith to our business life. Is it too much to hope that one day soon we may be able to eliminate the phrase "Christianity *and* business" and to say instead, "Christianity is *in* business"?

Faith-*fully and* practice-*ingly yours, etc.*

— 23 —

Mr. John Businessman
Everytown, U.S.A.

Dear Friends:

I hope you will all pardon this one mimeographed letter sent to each of you. Our separate and individual letters throughout the year have been a great source of delight as well as education for me. But now as the Christmas season approaches, I thought I would like to send you the same greetings, and, if you will understandingly accept it, a small sermonette. I do not write this as advice from on high, nor insult you with a moralistic plea to "put Christ back in Christmas," whatever that is supposed to mean. Rather, I should like to share with you what I believe is a common concern, one which has cropped up in some of your letters, one which we have not really dealt with, and one which certainly is of appropriate concern at any time in the year, but especially now.

We have written often about the nature of Christianity and how it can offer us some help and vital relation to our everyday business problems. But thus far, we have described sample applications only in terms of its relevance to each of us as individuals. We have more or less assumed that each of us, as individuals, are trying to take our Christianity seriously and responsibly. And while we have said that the Christian faith is both personal and social, we have left out all discussion of the Church. We did acknowledge quite early in our various letters that many of you feel that the Church has not offered you much, if any, practical help. Most ministers don't know much about economics, let alone the complex affairs of business. It is understandable why businessmen should feel that the clergy simply do not understand the kind of problems there are in the mercantile world. It is also true that many people are pro-Christian but anti-Church. This is usually expressed through the question, "Why can't I be a good Christian without going to church?"

My little sermonette, therefore, tries to deal with the problem of the Church. Let me begin by acknowledging all the weaknesses of the Church. There is no point in getting defensive about the sins of the Church. For every weakness the outsider can mention, we who are on the inside can name ten more. Since we are on the inside, we really know how bad it is and can be. Moreover, there are quite a few books out now which cast very severe and very detailed judgment on the institution. It is almost a vogue now to kick the Church. It is my conviction that we should accept these judgments with great seriousness and humility. They are true and there is no doubt that a very great and profound reformation of the Church is needed. So let us not waste time in arguing or in trying to counter the charges by listing some of the good sides of the Church.

My second point would be to suggest that the person who claims he can be a good person without going to church does not really understand either the nature of the Church or the nature of the faith. It is obvious that there are many relatively good people outside the Church. So let us not say that Church people are better than non-churchgoers. If there are good people outside the Church, let us give thanks to them and to God that this is so. Meanwhile, let us recall that the Church is for those who are not good enough, who know it, who confess it, and who want to be better. The Church is the one great institution in society which is based on failure. All other organizations are based on some criterion of success. The Christian Church's condition for membership is the acknowledgment that we are failures, that we are sinners who stand in the need of forgiveness, that we are people who cannot live life adequately on our own, that we need help and direction and power. That is one side of the story. The other side is that even if we have some measure of ability, success and love, then it is our responsibility to share it, to give it, to rededicate it. Precisely because the Church is so weak, it needs the help of people. The man who says, "I can be a good Christian without going to church," may be half right. But if he is so good and just and loving, then why doesn't he pitch in and help the rest of us struggling people? So long as he stays outside, claims goodness, I must question just how much responsible love he really has. If he is so loving, why not help this weak vessel of Christ?

My third point would be a gentle reminder that surely all of us in our correspondence have noted time and again the complexity and difficulty of ethical and moral decisions. All of us know the shades of gray choices, the awesome compromises, the mixtures of evil and good, and the struggle to even maintain a sensitive conscience and stable faith. Surely our daily life puts enormous burdens upon our powers to work for the most minimal justice and right decisions. Of course, I cannot speak for you, but for me, the demands of the Christian faith are exceedingly high, the temptations to water it down very powerful. Thus, my conclusion is that I cannot struggle alone. I need other people, their wisdom, their shared experiences, their insights, their ethical knowledge. Further, I need God's help, His wisdom, but most of all His forgiving grace and His love to impel me onwards. It is in the Church where one can find God and people of similar concerns. To use a somewhat crude, but I believe common and apt analogy, I would say that we are much like automobiles. We are wonderfully made with many fine powers and capacities, but we need regular refuelling and check-ups, and every now and then, we need a thorough over-hauling. We are a finely made machine and yet we are more than that. But even so, we cannot run by ourselves creatively.

And if we argue that the Church is not really doing its job of keeping us in shape, we acknowledge that this is largely true. Indeed, the Church is frequently only a kind of vague spiritual uplift society, or too social, or too irrelevant. But again, we shall have to assert that now is the time to change it. God and people are present in the Church. The problem is that we people, clergy and laity, have not done our job.

My fourth point is that we people can change our role in the Church and help make it more what it ought to be. It is important, I think, to realize that it is not the clergy alone who will effect any significant reformation. This is not to let us off scot-free. It is to acknowledge that we too need to reform ourselves. We need to listen long and seriously to you businessmen and your problems. We need to know more about economics and so on. We need to know how to speak to you in terms you can understand. We need to do a lot of other things, change some of our seminary education programs and teaching methods. But the main point here is that a real change must also come by and because of laymen. Somebody once said that "a minister is a lost layman." I take this to mean that it is the layman who is the heart of the Church. Therefore, this is where the real reformation must take place.

What does this mean in terms of practical action? I believe it means that it is time for you laymen to ask for and demand the changes. And most clergy would be delighted to oblige. For instance, ask that travelogues and magicians be eliminated from the Men's Club programs. Ask for study and discussion groups that deal with your business ethical problems. Request experts from the outside, if necessary. Be not afraid to deal with controversial questions and problems in economics and politics. Controversy and differences of convictions are part of life and they belong in the Church as well. There is a better chance of having controversy become more fruitful under the judgment of Christ, than over a bar or the back fence. Let us ask each other, clergy and laity, to spend more time in relating our faith to our life. This is our task and this is part of the nature of our faith and its Church. If "worship is practicing the presence of God," it is also the means whereby God enables us to have more power for living His will in our daily lives. But I believe it is also His will that we worship Him with our minds as well, and therefore seek to understand how to do His will where we work. If we do these things then we can become truly a people of God together, and ambassadors of Christ wherever we are.

Yours in the Church of Christ,

William A. Spurrier